final chapters

final chapters

writings about the end of life

EDITED BY ROGER KIRKPATRICK

FOREWORD BY JONATHAN DIMBLEBY

Jessica Kingsley *Publishers*
London and Philadelphia

First published in 2012 by Dying Matters Coalition

This revised edition published in 2014
by Jessica Kingsley Publishers
73 Collier Street
London N1 9BE, UK
and
400 Market Street, Suite 400
Philadelphia, PA 19106, USA

www.jkp.com

Copyright © Jessica Kingsley Publishers 2014
Foreword copyright © Jonathan Dimbleby 2014

Library of Congress Cataloging in Publication Data
Final chapters : writing about the end of life / edited by Roger Kirkpatrick.
    pages cm
"First published in 2012 by Dying Matters Coalition."
"Revised edition."
ISBN 978-1-84905-490-4 (alk. paper)
1. Death--Literary collections. 2. Grief--Literary collections. I. Kirkpatrick, Roger.
PN6071.D4F56 2014
808.8'03548--dc23
                              2013036540

British Library Cataloguing in Publication Data
A CIP catalogue record for this book is available from the British Library

ISBN 978 1 84905 490 4
eISBN 978 0 85700 886 2

Printed and bound in Great Britain

CONTENTS

❧

FOREWORD

☙

JONATHAN DIMBLEBY

Grief is an emotion so overwhelming and so intense that it is almost impossible to describe its meaning. Even if we do stumble across the words between our tears of sorrow or bellows of rage, we are so seared that we fear to burden others with our pain lest its intensity drives them away from us. Paradoxically, we may, at the same time, shy away from seeking to share our suffering in case it is diluted in the process, prizing us apart from the person we still love but who is gone forever. Moreover, the grief is ours, unique and precious. We do not want it contaminated by those who seek to console but to inadvertently say the wrong thing; whose well-meant clumsiness makes our isolation the more desperately complete.

I suspect, though I do not yet know, that awareness of one's own imminent death may arouse a similar range of complex emotions. It is our death, our loss, our fear. How can it be shared? How can anyone else even begin to understand? How do we protect those we love from the desolation of our departure?

It is hard if not impossible for many of us to talk about such matters. The statistics tell us that by the middle of this century the number of those living to the age of 85 or more will have quadrupled to four million. This wonderful fact has profound consequences collectively for British society and individually for us and our families. But the statistics also reveal that only one in three of us ever discuss the meaning of death with anyone else. Moreover a similar proportion of doctors never raise 'end of life' issues with their patients.

That is why *Final Chapters* matters. It demonstrates that even if we can't talk about it, we can write about death with astonishing power and eloquence. The poems and prose in this small volume are a revelation. Written by some who grieve and others who are close to death, they do not invite a casual skim. They are by turns raw and harrowing, wry and bleak. But they have in common a compelling honesty that is touching and illuminating.

The authors are men, women, patients, parents, sons, daughters, doctors and nurses. I imagine that in the writing they found a release for their own powerful emotions. But by sharing their experience they do their readers a very great service as well.

At some point we will all face that inevitable terminus, the end of life. I think you will find that by facing that implacable fact, *Final Chapters* makes this shared prospect less daunting and therefore, perhaps, more bearable as well.

Jonathan Dimbleby
Chair of Dimbleby Cancer Care

INTRODUCTION

છ

EVE RICHARDSON

Talking and reading about other people's childhoods, schooldays, separations, sadnesses and happiness help us to cope with our own ups and downs. But that kind of shared experience is seldom there to comfort and support us when our life is nearing its end or we have lost someone we loved, because most people don't want even to think about dying, let alone discuss it.

This reluctance, while understandable, is a massive barrier to receiving timely, dignified care and help towards the end of our lives, and makes it much harder to come to terms with death, which is as much a part of life as being born. Although someone in Britain dies every minute, many people risk missing out on having their end of life wishes met and leave behind a muddle for those close to them to sort out.

That's why the Dying Matters Coalition was set up in 2009 by the National Council for Palliative Care. With a fast growing membership which currently stands at over 30,000 including charities; services across health, social care and housing; care homes; hospices; funeral, legal and financial services; and a wide range of individuals, Dying Matters is at the forefront of changing attitudes and behaviour around dying.

We launched *Final Chapters*, our first ever creative writing competition, because we suspected that many people would find it less upsetting to write about dying than to talk about it.

We were proved right, and were delighted to receive almost 1,400 stories and poems. Parents, husbands, carers, children, partners, wives, grandparents, nurses, doctors, friends and dying people contributed from all over the UK and every continent. They testified to a common humanity. Their works speak of the profound emotions that come with living and the anxiety, anger, jealousy, acceptance, remorse, irreverence, grief and relief, as well as humour, engendered by love when it is worn raw by the ending of life.

The wide range encompasses an acceptance of mortality, an internal monologue on dementia, a pithy haiku on hypocrisy, a palliative care nurse's story, an account of digital mourning and the poignant narrative of one widow's day.

Certainties in life are few but dying is one of them. By talking about it more openly and taking actions such as writing a will, recording our funeral wishes, registering as an organ donor, planning our future care and sharing what we would want with our loved ones we can help to ensure that dying well comes to be seen as part of a good life.

I am only sorry that there is space in this collection for just a few of so many works we read with sympathy, enjoyment and admiration.

I hope that you find these stories and poems as moving as I have and that they spur you on to share your wishes with those close to you.

Eve Richardson,
Chief Executive,
Dying Matters Coalition and the
National Council for Palliative Care

LEAVE-TAKING

℘

HELEN BARNES

I've never known an autumn like it. The leaves still on the trees, not even changing colour till November. The flowers just went on and on, as the days got shorter. I saw the strangest sight – a rosebush covered with rosehips, dark red and shiny, and frail white blooms, papery in the evening light. And that's how it's felt for me too these last months; the past and the present vividly with me all at once. Endings. And beginnings – intense new friendships and conversations. Short-lived, but no less real for that.

And now spring is coming – so fast. I had thought it would hurt, knowing that I was seeing everything for the last time. And it's true that I can see everything more vividly than ever. Snowdrops, hellebores, that yellow-green wash of new growth on the weeping willow. But I am moving away from it all quite quickly now, detaching. I used to read the paper every day, watch the news. I can't be bothered any more; it seems like something happening on another planet. When people come to see me and talk about their news, it's hard to remember what it felt like – to care about jobs and children's successes, holidays and books.

In a strange way it reminds me of being pregnant, the body insisting on the primacy of its needs. The brute simplicity of surrender is almost a relief. And the other thing is the same too. The fear of the thing you have to do on your own; the looming ordeal you cannot avoid. But that becomes less frightening the less you resist, the more you hunker down into it, just listen and wait.

I remember an old man I used to know when I was growing up. He used to cut flowers from his allotment every week – dahlias in clashing pinks, maroons and yellows, bronze chrysanthemums – and carry them on the bus to the cemetery, wrapped in a sheet of newspaper. I like to think of my friends doing that for the funeral. The homeliness of it.

I won't be here for the roses. For cherry blossom or forget-me-not. But maybe one more time to see the bluebells, spilling out of the woods like floodwater; fallen sky.

THE NIGHT SHIFT THAT CHANGED ME

ℰↃ

ALEXANDRA OBEE

Sunday evening on a warm, May Bank Holiday. Beer gardens are packed with red-faced patrons, slowly sipping their cold drinks. Children play in the streets with excited smiles, knowing there's no school in the morning. The smell of barbeques fills the air and washing hangs, drying in the slowly fading sun.

This is what I see from my car as I drive in to work, bleary eyed. It's as if I'm watching it on television, the windows acting as a screen, separating me from the world outside and all the fun that's being had. Dressed as usual, in my smart work attire but with my comfiest shoes on my feet, I know it's going to be a long night. A seemingly endless day had been spent in bed trying to sleep, the sun's rays forcing their way through the thin blinds, invading every aspect of my broken sleep.

The junior doctor's best friend, caffeine, had been consumed in its various guises, tea, coffee, energy drinks, chocolate. But still I was tired.

This particular weekend though, the bleariness in my eyes wasn't only due to my confused circadian rhythm offset with high-sugar beverages. I had been crying. I had spoken to my Mother on the telephone and had realised that my Grandfather, who had been suffering from advanced lung cancer, was losing his long battle that night. The sound on the telephone of his breathing in the background was one I had heard many times before. The death rattle. Only, previously, it had been other people's relatives. I had had sympathy with the families at the time, of course, but it was different when it was my own, amazing, strong, stoical Grandfather.

I had a long internal battle with myself. Do I go to work? Do I race halfway up the country to be at his bedside? I had said my goodbyes in the preceding week, and I knew what my Grandfather, a miner with an intensely strong work ethic, would have wanted me to do.

So to work I went. Past the barbeques, the beer gardens and the playing children. Into the work car park, into the doctor's office to take the bleep from my colleague as I did at the start of every night shift.

But something was slightly different that night. I realised through the sadness of not being able to look after my own Grandfather that night, that I could look after other people's relatives and hopefully in doing so provide some comfort for them. This idea had always been in the shadows of my practice – I treated my patients with care, dignity and respect. But that night brought this thought to the forefront of my mind. Every patient I dealt with that night I thought of my own Grandfather. How would I want this patient to be treated if it was a relative of my own? Can I do a simple act of kindness like rearrange a pillow, or fetch an extra blanket? Should I go to the vending machine for yet another cup of treacle-like coffee after prescribing that paracetamol, rather than before?

In today's society we no longer live and work within a few streets of our most-loved family members. We work long hours, and may not be able to directly care for our relatives when they need it the most. The realisation of the privileged position I was in, being able to care for other people's family members, eased the pain of not being able to directly care for my own.

Early that same morning, as the sun was rising and flooding the dark wards with an orange glow, I felt the familiar vibrations of my mobile phone in my pocket. Phone calls at such a time fill most people with a sense of unease. That night

I knew what the phone call heralded. It was my Father, telling me that my Grandfather had passed away peacefully at home, with my Grandmother, his wife of 69 years, at his bedside.

That night had changed, in a small but important way, the way I practiced medicine. Missing out on the Bank Holiday festivities, the barbeques and the beer gardens was insignificant in comparison to being able to care for someone in need.

As junior doctors we can rarely cure, sometimes heal, often ease pain. But we can always care.

Treating each patient as if they were a member of my own family helps me to get through the long, unsociable hours and emotionally difficult situations we face every day. It makes the job of a junior doctor, in my opinion, one of the most rewarding jobs there is.

SWAN

❧

BRENDA READ-BROWN

I never expected this.
When they said a sense of loss
I imagined emotions would be torn and tossed
Internally, perhaps eternally across the days
And nights of waking; making you stay near
Would merely mean replaying pictures,
Saying your words again and again
Until the tape wore thin.

But
I miss you with my skin,
My guts; nerve endings
Damaged, needing mending,
Fingers as well as hopes forlorn, I mourn
You with my muscles and my bone.

I understand so well the widowed swan who swims alone,
For this is animal; the brutality
Lies in the physicality; the tangible reality
Of isolation slices limbs off life,
And when parts are missing there can be no re-creation
Of totality, or of sense.

Certainty can only ever be in the past tense,
And nothing was as known as this last nothing;
No touch of love more felt than this
Endless embrace of your absence,
And death's final
      insubstantial
        kiss.

AVA'S LOVERS

෴

CLAIRE JONES

In the slow, solitary hours of evening the gulf seems to widen between those of us who are living and those who are dying. Each quiet tick of the clock that pulls us up the long, slow path to morning holds something different for you than it does for me. Last night I slept for only a few hours. There's always a noise to disturb you here. I get out of bed at four and take my chair by the window to watch the dawn wash-out the night. As a young mother, I had often watched the morning come, holding Anthony in my arms. I used to marvel at my soft, new son and to plan our days. Those long, long days.

The morning comes slowly today. A December drizzle hangs low across the hospice grounds. Inside it is warm, but I pull my shawl closer. I am cold. At six the young nurse fetches me a cup of tea. Her unasked-for kindness breaks my solitude but I try to be grateful. Muted strip lighting springs to life defying the dull morning in the same way that other people try to defy the horror of my dying with their sad smiles and cups of tea.

The curtain is still drawn around the opposite bay. Perhaps today will be her day. She's been here as long as I have; we both came in on the twelfth of November. She introduced herself to me.

'I'm Ava.' She held out a bony hand.

'That's nice.' I said.

Her hair was long and dark, speckled slightly with grey and tied down in a low knot. She twirled the ends of it with ceaseless fingers. Her knees looked thin, even under layers of hospital blankets. She seemed fragile, faint as a breeze. Tears hung in the corners of her eyes and her plump lips turned down. She may well have been 40 but she cried softly like a little girl when her curtains were drawn. On the second day she caught my eye as the nurse plumped our pillows. She brandished a tatty *Closer* magazine at me. 'Would you like to borrow it?'

'No thanks,' I countered with a *Woman's Weekly.* She nodded and pressed her lips together.

Anthony visited me that evening to make small talk. He smiled hello at Ava and she beamed back, the life springing to her face. Once he'd drawn the curtain he motioned to Ava's bed and whispered, 'She seems nice Ma. What's she...why's she...?' he tailed off, aware of his indiscretion. We don't talk about that here. It might be cancer, heart disease, dementia; the list of foes is endless. We're all here for one journey, the vehicle is irrelevant. I had asked Anthony to limit his visits to twice a week, on the premise that it was a long way for him to travel. In truth his visits drain me. His need to see me, to hold onto me. The sadness in his face. It's all a bit much.

On the third day, Ava received a visitor of her own. A tall, elegant man strolled into the ward just after four. He had silver hair and smooth, brown skin. His expensive suit and shoes were set to stun but his face was crinkled in concern. He dropped three dozen red roses at Ava's feet and snatched up her hands.

'Oh Ava,' he sat on the edge of her bed, and pressed himself into the curve of her waist. 'Why didn't you tell me before now? Why leave it until...until it's...' he closed his eyes. I watched them intently over my Maeve Binchy.

'What would you have done, Marcus?' she freed one of her hands and cupped his face. 'It's been over for such a long time. I only wanted to say goodbye.' She peered into his face for a morsel of something. He shook his head.

'Don't, Ava. Don't...'

She clenched her teeth and smiled. 'I was hoping you might...stay? I don't think it will be long now.'

Marcus sat up a little straighter. 'Now Ava, you know I can't. I have to be in Paris this time tomorrow and you know how Helen is, I mean I couldn't put her through that again.' He lifted up her chin. 'You've always been such a beauty. I'm so sorry it's come to this.'

They stayed holding hands for ten minutes or so before he stood to leave, slowly freeing his hands from hers. 'Will you call Federico?' she asked. He nodded.

After he was gone, Ava leaned back into her pillows, pale but dry-eyed. I buried myself in *The Glass Lake* and asked the nurse to draw my curtain as she passed.

That evening Ava was wheeled away for treatment and I didn't see her until the following afternoon. Her eyes were sunken and her hair hung loose in greasy strands. I looked over but she rolled onto her side and curled around herself. From time to time her thin back shuddered under the weight of her grief. In the end, I turned away too.

By the time I got up the following morning, she was out of bed, hair clean and brushed, cheeks tinted with rouge. She sat reading and gazing out of the window until visiting time. I was ready with my *People's Friend* and a pen. At a quarter past the hour a young man burst through the double door. No roses, no suit. Instead he sported divine cheekbones and a definitive jaw. When he spoke his voice was heavily accented, Italian possibly, and very loud. I didn't have to strain to hear a single word he said.

'What the hell, Ava? You get that Marcus to call me? That jerk! Why you not call me yourself, huh? You walk out of my life and I think I never see you again and then this? To hear from *him*? What are you thinking?'

He paused and looked down at her shrunken frame, her pale face, her bony arms. A tear rolled down her cheek. The Italian crumpled, all rage gone. He plopped down at her feet. She took his head in her lap and whispered softly to him.

I saw him shake his head, 'I can't.' They sat together like that until the nurse came to announce that visiting time was over. As her Italian stood, Ava asked him once more.

'No, Ava. I'm not that man anymore.' He leant down and kissed her, a slow, wet kiss that even stirred something in my barren old soul. And then he left.

Each day was the same, a new visitor for Ava. Each time a different man. I noted them all down in the margin of my pocket diary. She had a different flavour of man for every day of the week. Once the list had reached 12, the visitors stopped coming and once the visitors stopped coming, Ava stopped getting out of bed. She would watch the clock from half-three in the afternoons, glancing at the double doors every once in a while. After three days with no visitors, Ava asked the nurse if she could make a phone call. The nurse wheeled her to the front desk and Ava dialled with trembling fingers. I heard her breath catch as the person at the other end of the phone answered.

She squeezed her eyes shut, 'It's Ava,' she whispered. 'Please come.'

After a minute she put down the receiver and the nurse wheeled her home. As Ava pushed herself up from the wheelchair she faltered, her skinny arms giving way and the nurse had to help her onto her bed. There wasn't much of her left. I glanced at the list I had made. It was entitled 'Ava's Lovers?' I had annotated each entry with tiny comments such as 'intense' or 'surely not?' but now, looking at her wasted frame I tore out the list and crumpled it into the bin.

Not one more visitor came for Ava until yesterday afternoon. She didn't even look up as the doors banged open, but I did. I saw him falter at the door, a tall, slim man in a crew-neck sweater. He held his body tightly and kept his face blank. His eyes found Ava and I saw him take a tiny bite of his lower lip. He didn't stay long. I heard Ava crying and saw her holding out her hand to him, but he shook his head and stayed out of reach. He studied the floor and kept his face closed. As he walked away Ava called after him 'Please, James. Please!' but he just walked away.

☙

And now, sitting in the gap between darkness and light, not sure which way I will go, I understand why Ava summoned her lovers. I see her time has come, her path is set. I slip my oxygen mask off as I push myself out of the chair. It takes me a while as I lumber around my own bed and through the curtain that surrounds Ava's. She lies in bed, a smudge of a person. I can hear her breathe, long slow pulls. And in these moments that separate Ava from the forever dark, I do the thing that none of her many lovers would do.

I hold her hand.

THE MILKMAN CRIED

❧

JOSEPHINE HOWARD

The milkman cried when I told him you were dead.
'Last night,' I said, 'Mark died.'
I remember still how rain beat down that day
As we stood at my back door,
And drops fell off the brim of his ancient hat.
I handed back your book of milk tokens.
'I won't need that now,' I said.
He touched my arm;
We cried together in the rain.

He made you gurgle with delight
Each Friday as he waited to be paid.
Played 'Peek-a-Boo'
While I hunted for my purse.
He asked if you'd been ill, I shook my head.
'I found him dead,' I said, 'in his cot.'
I paid the bill and watched him walk away,
His shoulders hunched against the rain.

'Cot death,' the coroner said.
Your little life snuffed out.
'Don't blame yourself.'

I keep your birthday cards safe, faded
Now after more than 40 years.
And photographs, in black and white,
A record of your days.
Years were spread before you, so I thought,
Time enough for you to live your life.
Grow, prosper with a wife and children of your own.
I've grown old while you are locked in time,
Still staggering your first steps.

JOURNEY'S END

☙

SUE MOORHOUSE

She lies in the bed that has been her home for over a year now. She is bone thin, unable to move. Her pain relief patch is in place, thank God. She is clean, warm, fed and there is evidence that frequent drinks are provided; the beaker of squash and syringe used to drip it into her mouth.

Journey's end, or should be. Sadly the ship is stuck in the doldrums, no wind, not even a ship's boat manned by a muscular crew to tow her onwards. She is T.H. Bundy to use the doctors' rumoured acronym. In other words totally helpless but unfortunately not dead yet.

She would be horrified if she knew.

It is hard to guess what she knows now. She doesn't speak or smile any more and it is years since she recognised anyone. Her eyes sometimes seem to focus on faces but only in the same way that a very young baby's do. Is she going backwards in time as more of her brain dies? Back towards infancy and beyond; a journey in reverse.

This particular journey starts with:

'Hallo, love, you're up early. I'm just going to make my breakfast.'

'Mum it's tea time. It's your afternoon nap you have just woken up from.'

There's no convincing her. It is not what her brain is telling her.

On her birthday she opens our card. I screw up the envelope but, no, she wants to put the card back into the envelope again. By then she has forgotten who it is from. She takes it out again and reads our names then looks at the crumpled envelope. 'That's typical of those two,' she remarks. We laugh for days afterwards.

The next small strokes take away her ability to stand and to sequence actions and take her into an anxiously chosen care home, specialising in dementia care. The journey progresses through terror and violent reaction: 'They're attacking me!' 'Get out, get out, the house is on fire!' 'For God's sake don't drink the tea!' The tea in question is being poured triumphantly into an armchair. *They* won't poison her, whoever *they* are. She is incredibly strong when she is frightened and angry, though she is frail. On really bad days she knows what is happening to her and remembers with horror that she has done something violent.

Sometimes she seems completely normal and asks after the family and how her cat is.

'How is James?' she asks. That's her son. He has been dead for ten years. After the first time, we don't tell her. She'll forget again, but she will suffer in that moment.

Her feet are off the ground. She's floating with no anchor, not remembering where home is. 'Can I come home with you?' she keeps asking and it makes us cry.

'You're just here to convalesce,' we lie. 'You'll be able to come home when you are better.'

She is reassured for a little while.

She has lost all chronological sense; any sort of logical sense for that matter.

She is 91 and she says she wants to go and live with her grandfather in Ireland.

She is crying, saying, 'My mother is dead.'

We tell her that it is very sad but it happened 40 years ago.

'No, no, I've just heard.'

She recognises her grandson when he visits. 'Is it really Daniel?' She smiles delightedly and banters with him just as she used to.

She often catches her breath on little sobs.

'I just want to sit and cry,' she says.

Today she is worried that her mother adopted her and was not really her mother. She was actually the child of an unmarried aunt.

We say, 'It doesn't matter as long as you had a happy childhood.'

'Oh, yes, I did, I did!' A smile.

Some days she seems well and we are happy.

'Shall we go over there and join in?' she asks. The other side of the room the residents are playing with balloons, tossing them on a sheet they all hold on to. This is so unlike her, we are thrilled.

There is a quiz going on. She seems to ignore it.

'A town beginning with L?' the question is.

'London,' she says suddenly, coming back briefly from whatever distant sea she has been drifting in.

She likes to hear about her new great grandson.

'I know there's a baby in my life somewhere,' she says.

We show her pictures. A month later we bring another photo of the baby standing up, but now she can't see it.

We jolly her along, planning trips to the seaside she used to take us to.

'Mind the buses,' she says when we leave promising to be back soon, and she waves. Looking back we see her staring blankly in front of her again.

For a while she knows that she recognises us but not who we are. Then she doesn't know us at all. She seems to be worrying less now but who can tell?

Now she has to move from a residential home to a nursing home. She lies in a bed with sides to stop her falling out. The door of the room is open and a radio plays for company. The good news is different at this stage of the journey.

'She ate a whole bowl of porridge today.'

'She likes her food mashed up not liquidised.'

'She seems more settled with the new pain relief patches.'

The best news is when she seems comfortable or is asleep when we visit. The carers are kind and conscientious but sometimes we can see that she is in pain, though she cannot express it in words.

We talk to doctors and nurses. 'We don't want her to suffer,' we say. It seems obvious to us that this is the priority now.

They explain about palliative care. They have to be careful with the morphine. We don't understand why. Her best friend, also 91, begs us. 'Don't let her be in pain!' Not keep her going for as long as possible at all costs. But don't let her be in pain. There is mutual incomprehension. What seems like humanity and common sense to us seems medically unprofessional to them. We feel powerless to help her. However much we protest, sometimes calmly, sometimes crying in spite of ourselves, we know that there are times when she will be suffering.

Death should not be a long drawn out form of torture. Her long journey should be over now. It should end in a gentle sleep.

HYPOCRISY

ೲ

SALI GRAY

The old woman died.
No helping hand in her life.
And now they all weep.

AN ORDINARY DAY

ლ

KYLIE JOYCE

An ordinary day; telly and tea, silence and solitude. He feels
the boredom already creeping into the drawn out minutes
but he has long since given up fighting it. He knows he
should do something different, surprise himself, shake off the
apathy. Every day he tries to make an effort but inevitably
feels his good intentions sneak off guiltily with each click of
the remote control. Maybe today will be different he thinks
half-heartedly.

He sighs and brings himself back to the task in hand.
Kettle on. The morning ticks on in its usual way, bowl of
cornflakes, morning radio, newspaper, postman delivering
the mail. It plops onto the mat with a satisfying thump. He
heaves himself out of the chair with a groan, wondering why
such simple things have become an effort. He pads slowly
over to the doormat, glancing at the small pile of envelopes
as he stoops to pick them up. He moves slowly back into the
kitchen, thumbing through the mail as he walks. A brightly
coloured envelope, offering a free packet of wild flower seeds
if he subscribes to their monthly magazine, catches his eye. He
might do that he thinks, attract some bees, do his little bit to
save the planet. There's a bank statement and a postcard from
Madeira which he'll save for last. The final letter makes him
pause; it is stiff, formal, with a franked stamp indicating the
Royal Free Hospital. He frowns slightly and his heart skips a
tiny beat. He decides on another cup of tea before he opens
it, unsure of his procrastination for he has been expecting

it; a letter confirming his follow-up appointment with the specialist.

He sits back down at the small breakfast table and fingers the letter in his hands. He notices their slight tremble but is unable to decide if it is nerves or his illness.

He tears the envelope open slowly, carefully and slips out the thick white folded paper.

His eyes scan the contents, pausing on certain words. His brain registers them, blanks out, restarts. It must be a mistake. Panicking now he reads the letter properly from the 'Dear Mr Reeves' to the 'Yours Sincerely Mr Paggett'. The words float out of the letter, hovering like black clouds, slowly filling the room: confirmation of recent examination, cancer, one year realistic. He feels stupid as he struggles to take it in. It doesn't make sense, the setting is wrong. Shouldn't he have been told this in person, in a warm and comfortable office, in front of a serious yet reassuring specialist? Not at his fading Formica breakfast table. Surely this isn't right?

Bitter nausea sweeps over him. He catches at the table, gripping the edges tightly, breathing deeply. Inhale, exhale. Realisation settles like a heavy cloak upon his shoulders. He has just been handed a death sentence with the morning mail.

He has no one to exclaim out loud to, to hand the letter to and ask them to read it. He must contain the shock and digest the awful truth alone. He feels faint. He looks around the room, expecting what? For something to register the horror that his life has just changed irrevocably. For the sky to turn black, for the sun to darken, for the radio to go silent. But of course nothing happens. Nothing except that for the first time in his life he can see the end of the journey he has been travelling on since he was born. The journey we all travel but don't always recognise the destination or acknowledge its end.

He feels changed. Suddenly his priorities are turned on their head. Not five minutes ago he was considering a subscription to a gardening magazine, now he might not be there to read the 12 monthly issues. He almost laughs at the irony. Almost, but tears of anguish seem to have swelled up of their own accord, forcing themselves out into the noiseless kitchen. They surprise him, shock him in their violence. He cannot remember when he ever cried like this before. Perhaps when his wife left him so unexpectedly. No not even then he thinks. But then he has never been told he has so little time left.

What will he do with it? He should make a Bucket List; that's the fashion these days. Yes he could visit the Grand Canyon, sky dive off Ben Nevis, see the sparkling glitter of Las Vegas. He considers his options; the world is his oyster! But when it comes to it he finds a very different list emerging; watch the birds feeding, fly his kite, listen to the football results, sip a pint in his local pub, enjoy a Sunday lunch. Suddenly it's all the small, insignificant things that mean the most. Insignificant things for an insignificant life he thinks hollowly, wondering where all the years have gone, what happened to his plans, aspirations, dreams.

He lets the thought go and considers his options, the time he has left on this planet. One year. It sounds pitiful, paltry, hardly worth the bother. He sips his tea wretchedly. One year...a little voice that has long been used to being ignored coughs quietly and makes itself heard the first time in years... it is also 52 weeks...or 365 days...or 8,760 hours...the voice whispers. Put like that it sounds abundant; plentiful. Some people live more in one day than others live in a week or a month. He considers this with slow deliberation, and feels a wave of determination whooshing joyfully through his veins, like an exhilarating fairground ride, as he makes a decision. He is going to be one of those people. And what's more he's going to begin this very moment. Right now. He laughs out loud; it feels odd, but good. He considers the things he wants to change, the people he wants to meet, reconnect with, laugh with. He has enough time left to make a difference.

It feels odd finding purpose in his life at the end of all things. But the thought gives him strength, calms him; he feels for the first time that he understands what it's all about. He sips his tea, appreciating the taste and temperature consciously for the first time. Delicious. He plans his day…let's see…he could drop in to see his elderly neighbour, see if there's anything he can do; oh, and he could stop by the Homeless Shelter and do a spot of washing up, they're always advertising for help. He could maybe have an iced-bun with the regulars, have a chat; then he could take a stroll through the park, throw soggy bread to the ducks, feed the birds, breath in the fresh air, feel the sun on his face. He feels happy that his morning is now filled with activities. He marvels at how easy it was.

But he knows it is not quite enough. He has a sudden urgent desire for people, his family, a wish to make amends for all the wasted time. He wonders if he should seize the moment and telephone his daughter, ask her if he can pop over. She has long since given up inviting him, defeated by his permanent non-attendance to family gatherings and Sunday lunches. It is time he made the 30 minute journey that has always seemed so much effort. He could take his kite; fly it with his young grandson. If she'll let him come. If the boy will want to. Nerves almost overcome him but he shakes himself, fuelled with quiet resolve. He has absolutely nothing to lose.

He digs out the number, ashamed that he doesn't know it by heart, settles himself into his armchair, takes a deep breath and dials the number. He hears the line connect, the ringing tone fills his ears, he hears it picked up and a soft familiar voice answers, 'Hello?' He pauses, 'Hello dear, it's dad.' 'Dad?' she sounds genuinely thrilled, delighted to hear from him, 'How lovely to hear from you. When are you coming over for a visit then?' He exhales and smiles, his heart warming and filling. 'Well, how about today, if you're around?' No time like the present he thinks, as he hears her delighted reply, and that's what it is for him now…a present.

GOOGLE MAPS SAVED MY LIFE

๛

ANNELIESE MACKINTOSH

He's in there, somewhere. Trapped, like a doll in a doll's house. Each time I switch on the computer, I create a new fantasy for him.

One day, I like to imagine he's listening to *The Archers*, cutting his nails over the bin. Another, and my mum's telling him off for putting an empty whisky bottle back in the cupboard. Another still, and he's teaching my sister to say 'turtle' in German, while she does cross-stitch at his feet.

Most often of all, I like to imagine that he's working on a long stretch of complex programming code, with two cups of lukewarm coffee beside him, and *Desert Island Discs* playing softly in the background.

But on this particular day, when I switch on the computer, I decide to play out something entirely new.

๛

You know those dreams where you can just click your fingers and time stands still? Where everything in the world freezes, except you?

And you can weave
            in and out of it all
        unnoticed
            for as long as you like
    until you click your fingers –
    and time carries on again just as before.

You'll have seen it on TV and in films. An early example occurs in *The Twilight Zone*, back in 1961, in an episode called 'A Kind of Stopwatch'. The protagonist, McNulty, owns a special watch that can pause time. More recently, it happened in that Tim Burton movie, *Big Fish*, at the moment where Ewan McGregor's character spots the love of his life.

You may have seen it in books too. There's that H.G. Wells story 'The New Accelerator', for instance, about a drug that causes you to move so fast that everyone else appears still.

Well, I've witnessed this freezing-time effect first-hand.

ᘒ

The first time I visited, it was out of homesickness. More than homesickness, I guess. Grief. Which is a type of sickness too.

I typed in the postcode and looked at the map. I zoomed in once, then again, and suddenly I was standing outside my old house: Chimney Cottage. It had been my family home for 24 years, and I knew every stain on the brickwork.

It was a bright day. Most of the trees had leaves on, and the sun was high in the sky. The wheelbarrow rested against the side of the house, and there was washing hanging on the line, fluttering in the breeze. All in all, it looked like a lovely spring afternoon.

I turned down the lane to get a better view of the front garden. The first thing I saw was the milk by the gate, not yet taken inside. And then I spotted the old sun-lounger. Just the skeleton, no mattress, sitting on the front lawn.

This told me something very important.

Dad wasn't dead yet.

Whatever moment in time this set of pictures was taken, the disease hadn't yet spread to my father's spine. I knew this because as soon as it did, the first thing he did was move the sun-lounger to the patio at the back of the house. He'd use his Zimmer frame to get from his bed to the back door, then he'd sit on the lounger and get some fresh air.

I began to look for other clues. The windows all looked pretty dark and impenetrable, but I zoomed in on each one, just to make sure. The first two were pitch-black, and contained nothing. But when I closed in on the third one, at the top-right of the house, I saw the outline of a jewellery box.

At the point that this picture was taken, then, Kit was still living at home. Which was over three years ago. Which meant my sister hadn't yet moved in with Gaz, which meant she hadn't yet become engaged, which meant she hadn't yet tried to slit her wrists in the bath.

I moved further down the lane and looked onto the driveway. One silver car; one red. So at the very moment this picture was taken, Mum and Dad were both at home.

'Hello!' I called. 'Mum! Dad! Kit! Are you there?'

I wanted to shake my computer until they fell out.

❧

Naturally there are limits to the zoom function on Google Maps. But the longer I stared at my house, from every angle I could get at it, the more easily I began to imagine myself opening a door and stepping inside. As if I was really there, and the house was really there, but it was just that time had stood still.

I tried to picture each member of my family; what room they might be in, what they might be doing at the exact moment the photo had been taken.

Mum was probably in the lounge, lying on the sofa in front of *Murder She Wrote*. Or, since it was lunchtime, maybe she was in the kitchen making parsnip soup, paused in a freeze-frame just as the wooden spoon had reached her mouth.

Kit would most likely be in her room. She usually hid in there, sitting on the floor doing craft. I could see her now too, midway through stuffing a felt frog, with a strange, sad darkness in her eyes.

And Dad? Well, Dad was in his office. No question. If only the camera had been able to travel around to the back of the house, I'd be able to see him sitting at his computer by the window, his fingers midway through pushing down the letters 'a' and 'n' on the keyboard. Yeah, Dad was in there alright.

My whole family was inside this magical puzzle.

&

It became a sort of habit, I guess. An addiction. I went back to look at the house every day, and would spend ages and ages just gazing at it, imagining what everyone was doing.

Remembering.

The mothball smell in the porch. The Wellington boots by the back door. The crumbs in the bread bin. The poppies on the bathroom tiles. The light bulb that never got replaced on the stairs.

This place where my dad wasn't about to die. Where he and my mum weren't afraid to sit within the same four walls as one another. Where my sister hadn't been committed to psychiatric hospital, and where everyone was doing okay, and nothing truly bad had ever happened to us.

&

Today, as usual, I zoom in on the sun-lounger in the front garden. And that's when I allow myself to play out a new fantasy.

What if today, I think, Dad is doing something different?

Today, he is writing me a letter. On his screen it says something like this:

My darling daughter,

This is the hardest letter I have ever had to write.

But before I die, I need to tell you how much you mean to me.

Ever since the day you were b

And at this exact moment in time, the exact moment that Google once chose to drive their camera-topped car through a hamlet in Buckinghamshire, my dad had been frozen mid-sentence, writing a message just for me.

I stand in the doorway, watching, willing him to come back to life and finish the letter.

But I know that's impossible.

Even if he was to come back to life, he wouldn't finish it. He'd sigh, he'd wipe away his tears, and he'd press backspace until it ate up every word on his screen. Then he'd go back to that long, complex code, because it was so much easier, so much less painful.

Eventually, I tiptoe away.

ↄ

You know, in just about every example, in those books and films where time stands still, there are always repercussions. In 'The New Accelerator', the drug causes your heart to beat so fast that you could die at any minute. In *Big Fish*, after time has stood still, it 'moves extra fast to catch up'. And in *The Twilight Zone*, perhaps most frightening of all, McNulty's stopwatch breaks, and time remains frozen for eternity.

ↄ

I look again at that empty sun-lounger in the front garden, and then I zoom out. From the dark, yellow vein of the A-road running alongside the house, I zoom out again. And again. Until I am staring at the Earth from space.

I think about particles and waves and movement and energy, and all the things my dad used to teach me about when I was a little girl. If everything in the universe were to pause, I think, there would be no light.

So I take a deep breath and switch off my computer – and time carries on again just as before.

BENEATH THE BRACKEN

(For K.M.)

᭟

JANETTE AYACHI

Your coffin a locker of broken microphones
cables circled the knuckles
of loved ones that lowered you,
eight chords, eight hands, eight bowed heads,
each body an amp for your voice
but something was wrong with the connection.
I tossed soil through white noise
its granolithic blend stuck to my cuticles
and filtered the first layer of darkness.
We buried you at the foot of the Campsie Hills,
rain paused, birds sang elergies, mud coated my shoes.
Later at the 'Drookit Dug' we played the jukebox,
this was where you drank and sang your life into memorial
following your heart and piercing holes in your liver.
The fabric of the seats unthreaded to sponge
the same colour your face was near the end.
Your lover in his over-sized suit counting the years
on his fingers, mixing tears with whiskey.
The hidden lovers warned to stay away,
as local drunks spilled pints and potent legacies.
What a turn out your last dance,
the stiff procession of red felt hearts
pasted on to black mannequins, they leaked
out over the church like an army flagging
your 'Requiem Mass' in grim tribute.
When they emptied your flat they found:

bank statements, the clothes of three different men,
photographs, letters, sheet music, empty wine bottles,
perfume and your son. These were the things
you left behind. Ghosts in the stairwell
songs trapped in the walls.
The only thing they forgot to disconnect was your phone
its siren rang in the empty room for days.

COAT HANGER

 handtitle

ADAM LOUND

Jean is up at dawn to take the dogs out walking. She invites me along. I groan as I turn away from her. Before she has even left the room I have pulled her side of the duvet towards me, hugging it for its warmth. Over the past few weeks there has been a dull grey transition out of autumn and into winter. My body seems part of the change. It aches. I curse the alarm. After pressing snooze several times I count up to 10, then 20 and then sigh and get out of bed. My eyes open as soon as my feet come into contact with the icy cold bathroom floor. The warmth of the shower is glorious. I could stay here forever. I take a moment to look at myself in the mirror while shaving. I've certainly grown better with age. My 55-year-old face is weathered and wise. My best feature is my thick grey hair. I think it gives me a look of distinction but I have to keep this thought to myself as hair is something we don't talk about in my family. My son Roy is going bald at an unprecedented rate. Jean is grey but dies her hair black and we all have to play along. Marie is desperately upset after each haircut she gets. She prefers visiting the dentist.

As I get dressed I look through the bedroom window. I see Jean returning with the dogs. Their breath condenses in the cold morning air. Although she can't see me I wave to her. My knees and the stairs creak in competition as I make my way down to the kitchen. I can hear barking in the garage. I take my pills with a glass of water. Blood pressure and cholesterol, the usual for a man my age. On my way out I lean into the doorway connecting the hallway to the garage. Jean is facing away from me filling up the water bowls. I say goodbye. She turns briefly, her face a flush of red, "Take your coat!" I find it on the rack at the front door. It's the first time I've worn it this year.

I push my hands deep into my pockets as I walk to work. The wind is cruel and manages to find its way through to the small areas of exposed skin around my wrists and neck. I never quite warm up again in the office. It's a slow day. All day. The sun doesn't makes it out from behind the clouds and at ten past five, feeling as if I have achieved nothing, I am back out into the oppressive wintery darkness making my way to see Dr Greenwood.

I've been visiting his surgery for so long that the receptionist always gives me his final appointment slot of the day and knows that I'll always manage to be late for it. The other doctors keep later, more convenient hours but they're young, aloof and inconsistent. Dr Greenwood is old fashioned. Thorough. He's brought me in to discuss a recent blood test. I have them on occasion to make sure I'm on track with my medications. I've known Dr Greenwood for over 30 years. He knows me. He knows my body and my family. So when he opens the door, shakes my hand and says, "Bill, it's good to see you," I know he means it.

I walk into the familiar office. I take my coat off and place it on the back of the chair. Behind me I can hear Dr Greenwood lock the door. Why did he do that? He's never done that before. He walks to his side of the desk and motions for me to sit first. I can feel the air slowly escaping the leather seat as I descend. He opens my file. He asks about Jean and then Roy and then Marie. He nods his head slowly as I speak but doesn't look up. He is using a fountain pen, the kind you need to keep moving because the ink flows out so freely. But he's not moving it. A blotch forms on the paper.

He looks up, "What about you? How are you doing Bill?" I say that I'm fine. He smiles at me. A sad smile. Is it pity?

He blows on the blotch of ink and once it has dried he begins flicking slowly through the notes. I've been here so many times over the years that he has quite a dossier on me: Ingrown toenails, bronchitis, kidney stones, stomach ulcers, eczema, arthritis as well as some pretty intimate details about my bowels and my bladder. "We've known each other for a long time Bill…" I get the impression he wants to say something more but instead he continues to slowly turn the pages. "Now let's have a look at these test results." He turns to his computer and looks over his glasses at the screen. Squinting, he types in my details. I've never seen Dr Greenwood this tense. His whole posture is taut. I can't help but think about the locked door. He clicks his mouse and the test results start printing. It is at this moment I realize that I'm holding my breath. The artery in my neck is pulsing. It seems my body realized before I did that something terrible is about to happen.

Dr Greenwood places the results on the desk in front of him. I guess deep down I knew this day would come. It's been like an ache in the back of my mind. Distant drumming. Cancer. My father went through this. I guess that's the way it works. Genetics. A family tradition, a heritage. My father succumbed to it and it was awful but he was 73. I'm only 55! Isn't each generation meant to live a little longer?

I think about our kids. We always talk about how well they're doing and they *are* doing well. Grown up. Married. Sorted really. They don't need me anymore. It's the life cycle. I just happen to be at the end of it, I realize that acutely now. But Jean, my dear Jean. She'll be devastated. She'll want something to blame. Smoking. She'll blame smoking. She'll feel guilty because she didn't agree to move to the countryside. Most of all she'll be scared. I'm scared. It is within this feeling of terror, with my pulse racing and my palms sweaty, that I remember the sensation of falling in love with Jean. That giddy, uncontrollable joy. That tremendous lightness of being. Although what I'm experiencing now is a different emotion, it is equally powerful. It's as if these feelings share a common frequency. Perhaps they're bound by their intensity.

I recall our brief goodbye this morning. We barely looked at each other. It seems such a waste to have left the house this morning not having held her in my arms. Why didn't I get out bed with her and walk the dogs? Why don't I spend every moment I can with her making sure every single second counts? It's because time has never been finite until this very instant. From now on it will be running through my fingers. Every clock I see will be counting down. I try to think about our relationship. Moments of love and understanding but all I can manage is the brief flash of her face as she turned away from me this morning. All I can hear is the sound of her voice telling me to take my coat and the silence that followed. It's as if I'm stationed, static in this moment. It's all too brief and unsatisfying. The world feels like it has suddenly expanded and I'm not sure if I'll ever make it home to see her again.

Dr Greenwood looks up. I guess I'm glad he's the one to tell me the news. It seems right this way. His voice shakes as he speaks, "Your sodium is a little high. Cut down on the salt. Otherwise your tests were normal. Just fine." I let out the breath I've been holding. I look for some kind of sign but nothing has changed. The sadness remains on his face. He places the results in my medical notes and pushes them to the far corner of his desk. He looks at me one more time as if he wants me to say something. I say, "Thank you."

Dr Greenwood then reaches into his bottom drawer and brings out two tumblers and a bottle of whiskey. A good one. Single malt. He pours a portion into each glass and slides one of them across the table towards me. He holds his glass with both hands in his lap. He looks down into the auburn liquid and he says, "I'm dying Bill." The traffic in the street fills the room. I can hear children fighting outside. A construction worker has started using some kind of drill, it makes a piercing shriek. It seems the whole world has been spurred into action by this single line.

"I've got cancer. It's spread fast. I wanted to tell you as you've been a patient for so long. I feel you should know this." He takes his whiskey in one gulp. I mumble, "I'm sorry" and then take my whiskey. It fills my mouth. I want to keep it there forever so I don't have to say anything as inadequate as "sorry" ever again. If he wasn't my doctor I'd ask him if he could get a second opinion? Or if there were any other treatment options? If he wasn't a doctor I'd tell him not to overreact. Not be so negative. But there is nothing I can do or say to help this man. If he knows it's bad then it's bad and that's that. "I finish up at the end of the week, after that I give myself three months max." I swallow the whiskey, concentrating on the warmth it creates in my chest. I have nothing say. Instead I stand and I shake his hand firmly and look him directly in the eye and I hope that this gesture gets across whatever it is that I should be saying. He places the whiskey and the glasses away in his drawer and leads me to the door. He looks at me one last time. A strong, confident look. He unlocks the door and pats me on the back as I leave.

I walk through the waiting room and out of the surgery. The brilliant intensity of the outside world hits me. I am alive and the feeling is overwhelming. I stop. I close my eyes. I attempt to take in each sensation individually. I breathe in the cool air. I try to separate the sounds of cars and conversations. I slowly open my eyes to a parade of colours and lights. It is then that I notice two things. I notice that I'm shivering. I'm absolutely freezing cold. I also notice that someone is calling my name. It's Dr Greenwood. He's running towards me. He seems excited, he's smiling. Was there some kind of mistake? It is then that I notice one more thing. He's holding my coat.

CHUBBY LITTLE CHEEKS

ༀ

SARAH BAKEWELL

Here he is. He's perfect. My little boy, my first child, my son. Here in my arms. I could hold him forever. All the pain I experienced bringing him into this world is now irrelevant, forgotten. I'm engulfed by love. I feel nothing other than love for my baby boy. My surroundings have faded into nothing; they do not matter. Nothing matters other than him now.

He has a mop of thick, black hair, like his father. His small eyes are shut, but he has beautifully long eyelashes. I long to see his eyes, no doubt they will be as perfect as the rest of him, but I dare not disturb him simply to see whose eyes he has inherited; grey-green, like mine, or bright, sparkling blue, like his father? He has an adorable button nose with a tiny beauty spot just underneath his left nostril. His ears are quite dainty. He has a small closed mouth and chubby little cheeks. His baby skin is so new and fresh, so smooth. He smells delicious. I hold him close to me.

He has five perfect fingers on each squishy hand, and five tiny toes on each miniature foot. So delicate and fragile. His perfectly formed arms lay crossed on his rounded stomach underneath his blanket. He has inherited the long leg gene of the other males on my side of the family.

My baby is beautiful. He is perfect. His eyes remain shut.

My surroundings slowly begin to drift back into place as muttered conversation disturbs the peaceful world which only my son and I share. I want to look up and shout at whoever has interrupted such a precious moment but I cannot take my eyes away from my son. How can I look away? My anger is washed away in an instant; I continue to stare at him. His eyes do not flicker.

I steal away from thoughts of my son growing up and try to re-piece my scenery, although I do not remove my eyes from my baby. I am still in my hospital bed in a delivery room. It is dark outside – I cannot remember if it was light when I delivered my baby. I could have been sat here silently for hours, just holding my son. I recognise the hushed tones of my husband near the foot of my bed and a female voice I do not. Perhaps the midwife is still here? I can't think why she would be.

I think of my son's room waiting for him at home. My husband's study is now barely identifiable; a shade of canary yellow occupies the previously cream walls, with an additional colourful border of farmyard animals. The small wooden cot situated against a wall adjacent to the window is filled with soft toys and blankets. A baby monitor is attached to one of the bars with its partner on my bedside table. The shelving unit opposite the cot, once home to my husband's various work-related files, folders and papers now stores nappies, dummies, clothes, bottles, bibs… Anything my baby could need. The room needs to have a baby in it.

'I'd like to take him home now,' I say quietly but firmly, still not taking my eyes off him. A heavy silence fills the room. I hear the slow, steady footsteps of my husband as he walks up to the head of the bed where I sit in my hospital gown, propped up by two pillows, holding his son. Our son. My son.

'Darling…' he struggles to find any more words, so instead, places a hand on my shoulder and gives it a squeeze. I painfully tear my gaze away from my son to look up at my husband. His usually bright blue eyes have lost their sparkle. They glisten with tears. They look sore, as if he's been crying for some time. He looks distraught, exhausted and apologetic.

'I'd like to take my son home now, please,' I say to him calmly, looking deep into his magnificent blue eyes before turning my attention back to my baby. He hasn't moved.

'I'm so sorry,' whispers the midwife, 'but you can't take him home.'

I look up at her, suddenly furious, cradling my son tightly to my chest. Who is she to deny this simple wish? I study the woman who believes she can prevent me from taking my baby home. She is a plump woman, rather short, with tight mousey brown curls. She too looks as though she has been crying. A tell-tale tear escapes from one of her small puffy red eyes and glides silently down her rosy cheek. I am his mother. And I want to take him home.

'He is my baby. My son. He's coming home with me.'

'Sweetheart…' begins my husband, but again words fail him. He eventually settles with, 'I'm so sorry.'

I look from my husband to the midwife and back again, then I look at my baby boy again. He lies in my arms perfectly still, in the same position as before. His eyes are shut.

I cannot let go of my son. How can anybody seriously suggest that I leave him here? I'm his mother. He is not staying here. I need him. I love him. He is mine. My perfect little boy.

They've given up. I have not. I can't let him go. He is mine; he grew from nothing inside me. I felt him moving and wriggling and kicking. They don't understand.

Since he was born, he has not opened his eyes, nor moved, nor cried. My newborn baby has not cried. He never will. I will never hear his cry. He will never look at his mother. He will never open his eyes. My perfectly formed, beautiful baby boy does not have a heartbeat anymore. His first breath will never come. I cannot let him go, because I'm afraid I will never hold him again.

I cradle my baby tightly and cry.

NAMES HAVE BEEN CHANGED

❧

CAROLE MANSUR

I went to see her yesterday. I keyed in the code, signed the visitors' book and climbed the stairs. I never use the lift although it would leave me right outside her room. I prefer to walk along the corridor, past the row of identical doors, and take an inventory, to see if they're all still there, in body at least. They lost their minds, a neuron here, a neuron there, long ago. When the name plate outside the room is bare, the photo vanished, it means the occupant, the service user – a Dolly or a Harry, a Dora or a Stanley – has died. Soon enough a new name – a new Dolly or Harry, Dora or Stanley – appears. A new old face, holding the camera's gaze for a moment, is affixed and everyone else shuffles along in the queue, like planes taxiing to the runway, waiting for takeoff.

The departures are never broadcast. It's very hush-hush. But in the first few hours afterwards, if you look into the eyes of the nurse or carer who was there, you can discern that as they sat by the bedside, holding a hand, they were on the threshold of other worlds. There are less subtle signs, too: a sudden clump of pensive relatives outside a closed door; an out of hours doctor, his briefcase snapped shut, signing a death certificate; an undertaker, dressed like a sommelier, emerging from the lift with a body zipped into a canvas bag, for all the world like a suit bag, upended on a trolley because there isn't room for it any other way.

She has spent a lot of time waiting, all told: waiting for the bus, which often never came; waiting for the kettle to boil;

waiting for the weather forecast or the nine o'clock news; waiting for us to come home from school; waiting for us to phone; waiting for milkman, postman, plumber; waiting for the rain to stop or the sun to shine and the washing to dry; waiting to die. She spoke about her own dying only once, long before the round of doctor's surgeries and the revolution of meals on wheels and Monday to Sunday dossette boxes began. She told us that she had written her will and deposited it in the safe at the bank; so we would know where to find it. The deaths of others, those she had outlived, were also given short shrift. She talked peevishly of her dead friends as if she had been abandoned at the end of a party, left alone amid the drained glasses and wrinkled balloons.

Dementia is a long final chapter. It is dying in very slow motion. In the departure lounge of the care home, with its circle of chairs, its rattling tea trolley and its singalongs, they sit for hours, even years. They will forget that last week's cabaret turn ended with Vera Lynn's 'We'll meet again' just as this week's did and the one a year ago and the one a year before that. They rise cautiously from their seats and hobble from handhold to handhold, table to rail to chair again. Their stiff, ancient limbs are eased onto forgiving cushions. Trembling hands dip towards the biscuit tin. The lounge is made cosy with flowers, prints of still lifes, an ominous clock. But this copy of a homely sitting room is made strange by an encumbrance of bewildering hardware: a hoist, that might be on secondment from an RAF sea rescue helicopter, there to lift the large Harry to the safety of his wheelchair; a congestion of walking frames in a nest of metal; a speak-your-weight chair reminiscent of death row.

Yet these somnolent last pages have dramatic interludes. I sometimes arrive in the middle of a territorial dispute of astounding verbal ferocity. 'That's my chair!' shouts the stalwart Dolly. 'I'll sit wherever I bloody well like,' Dora, a newcomer, puts it mildly. 'What about my leg?' retorts Dolly. 'I've got my tea and I'm drinking it. I'm not getting up. So bugger off!'

Then 'Shut up the lot of you!' comes a shriek from a previously comatose corner. As the day passes away, and body clocks begin to stutter, there are also physical assaults with Zimmers locked in combat like the horns of fighting stags. So seemingly frail, so seemingly tranquillised, these elderly citizens are far from docile. They are as embattled as anyone said to be 'fighting' cancer, in the time honoured martial cliché, although they're not granted the same heroic status. Obituarists will never write that they died 'after a long battle with dementia'. Left to fade away, lost in fogs of misunderstanding, they have to use whatever means they can to affirm 'I am still here', because the disease dismantles everything that tells them who they are.

They arrive in their bodies. They travel light, like wartime evacuees, with a suitcase packed with a few clothes. (If anyone asks, 'Did you pack this yourself?' The answer is, almost certainly, 'no'.) It is all that is left. Fifty years' worth of a family's accumulated paraphernalia she has left behind, 50 years' worth of stories. We turn out wardrobes and drawers, cupboards and shelves, sorting the detritus of a life that isn't quite finished but has no need for sherry glasses or sealing wax. Nor cake tins, brown paper, seaside knickknacks, knitting patterns, encyclopaedias, Royal Wedding souvenirs, theatre programmes, brooches, photographs – snaps she called them, school reports, Christmas decorations, hats. From all this we salvage but a smattering for her last room: a vase, a mirror and a pale lilac candlewick bedspread. The first time I put flowers in the vase, she stares at it. She recognises where it comes from. 'That's mine,' she says. 'That's from home.' A pause: 'No one's there, are they? The house is empty.'

She is still making connections then, and in some small corner of her mind she is in mourning for her former life: for the view of the flowering cherry tree in blossom, perhaps, or the sounds of milk bottles plonked on the step; a chuffing kettle; the radio's drone. A bereavement counsellor might suggest tying the worry of property ownership to a balloon and letting it fly away. For already, whips of prickly pyracantha are scratching the window panes. Spiders are threading cobwebs between the chair legs. Behind the front door, under the letter box, rises a tide of freesheets, flyers for pizza takeaways and estate agents touting for business. Her home is now merely a house. Material possessions and the identity they embodied have been shed. That chapter is closed. Her affairs are being put in order. The limits of existence are shrinking and will shrink further until she is curled, embryo like, in the hospital-issue bed under the lilac candlewick bedspread. The mental space she occupies now is as narrow as a window ledge, where she is pressed by the flames of the disease that will eat up all memory, not just the sepia tints of the past but the memory of how to walk, speak, even eat. We stand helpless below, looking up at the stick-like figure, and try to talk her into staying, not to give up, while knowing that there will come a time when the only course is to jump.

In the meantime she stretches out a hand towards whoever is within reach. 'Do I know these people?' she asked early on, a little imperiously. The man in the hat, dozing; the woman clutching her handbag; the pair who pace up and down together looking for the way out. She has never learnt anyone's name, either fellow travellers or staff. But she notices them. Vivid colours draw her eye: the sky is blue, the Wimbledon grass is green; her hair is black; his shirt is bright white. Even though I grow fond of them, these are strangers who share the end of her life. Each has a hidden past of which little seeps out. Behind the vacant faces, unfocused on the television, twiddling with paints and crayons, distractedly singing old hits, lie busy individual histories. Now they are tired, and they deserve the tranquillity of not watching the television, of not joining in.

They have little in common, apart from a ticket to the same destination. The disease takes a different path in every one of them. Yet each has outbursts of clarity: 'I've had a good life.' 'I never thought I'd end up here.' 'When am I going home?' And then, quite often: 'I'm frightened.' 'I'm frightened,' is a remark inviting the consolation of a squeeze of the hand or a caress of the cheek. Has the empty place at the table not gone unnoticed after all? Is the mood a deeper existential angst about the future, about what lies ahead, next month, next week, this afternoon, after life?

On her behalf, we have given some thought to the future. In the filing cabinet in the office at the care home is the End of Life plan. Who to telephone, in order (mobiles and landlines); then tick the box: home or hospital? Burial or cremation? As for when will it happen, and how, there can only be a gaping blank. There is something more we can do, though: in a recession, we read, funeral plans are booming. So on a sunny August day we visit the funeral directors and draw up an inflation-proof funeral plan, paying by instalments. A smiling woman in a colourful print blouse and cream trousers welcomes us. Her previous clients, a garrulous family, are about to leave: they are wearing jeans and trainers; while for this dress rehearsal we have chosen sobriety, jackets and polished shoes despite the heat. Decisions are taken swiftly with clear heads: it is easier to contemplate the colour of the coffin lining (we opt for cream; it goes with everything) now rather than later; and what to do with the wedding ring (we shall keep it). The mileage to the chapel of rest is computed, while 32.7 miles away she is having seconds of rice pudding. 'Are you sure you don't want a limousine?' The funeral consultant is vexed about the matter. 'If you change your minds about the limousines…'

Yet we will never be quite ready. Before a wedding, attendance is required at marriage preparation classes; before a baptism, there are baptism classes; before a death, there are only the practicalities of burial plots and hymns to discuss. The last rites come too late. The bereavement counsellor might as well be stuck in traffic. Back at the home, an undistinguished building with no architectural accolades (it's not a cancer centre; Maggie doesn't live here) we sit by the window to watch the passers-by, with their carrier bags of groceries, their push-chairs of children and their dogs. No one pauses to look up and wonder. No one in the living stream stops to acknowledge that in this graveyard in waiting, with its howls of anguish and the answering calm of the angel-carer, is a lesson in what it means to be human, a lesson in both frailty and strength. They walk on by, as long as death is an abstraction, until the day arrives when they key in the code, sign the visitors' book and climb the stairs.

Only the dying of others bequeaths the gift of foreknowledge. They leave an imprint. The world is different from the day before. There and not-there; presence and then, for all that we can see, absence. A lifetime ago, we travelled to my father's funeral in a limousine. Long and sleek, black and mournfully slow, driven by a solemn, voiceless young man whose blue-grey eyes staring into the mirror caught mine, the red rimmed eyes of a child. Among the belongings we found in my old bedroom drawer when we emptied the house was a black georgette headscarf worn just once, that funeral day, with a grey school coat. My mother must have thrown away the coat, but she kept the scarf. I shook the gauzy material, like a conjuror's handkerchief, and the memories spilled out: the sorrowful row of aunts adjusting hats and black gloves before the mirror in the hall. How smooth the centuries old wood of the pew had felt when we knelt to pray. How fast fading the gaudy flowers on the next door grave. How effortful the pall bearers who strained to lower the coffin into the deep trench; how light the pitter patter of soil cast on top.

My mother has forgotten even her husband's name. We have to do the remembering for her. But we shall not change our minds about the limousines. I do not wish to be reminded of a solemn young man's blue-grey stare.

When I am at home alone, when it is beginning to grow dark and afternoon is shading into evening, at that 'what's next?' time, I hear in my head the distant ringing of a phone. She is calling once more. I picture her in the gloaming half-light of her dining room, overlooked by tall cypresses planted long ago by my father. She steadfastly waits for me to answer.

She may say: 'Have you any chocolate?' I tell her to look in the pantry. She may say: 'I've lost my glasses.' I tell her to look in the fridge, because that is where they were found last time. 'Just a minute…just a minute…' Asperity tinges her still firm voice. She lays down the receiver and there is the familiar sound of her heels – not high, but not flat, rat-a-tat-tatting over the kitchen tiles. The same unmistakable tread I used to hear when she returned home with the shopping along the narrow lane next to the garden where I would be playing. She would unpack the bags and begin to cook. I could see her face flickering in the window as she stood peeling potatoes over the sink. And she saw me, her daughter, turning cartwheels on the lawn.

The night staff begin their shift at ten. I go to bed, placing the phone within reach beside me.

LET WINTER COME

☙

NICK JARVIS

Let the harvest fill the tables,
let the fields look a little lost,
let the flowers go to bed.

Let the days be undone by darkness,
let the trees shake off the last of their leaves,
let the rains wash the year away.

Let the puddles freeze,
let the moon rise and the snow fall,
let the sounds release their silence.

Let the children build their snowmen,
let the paths remain unswept,
let the drift pile up at the door.

Let the hinges squeak,
let the locks rust,
let the tools lie in their box.

Let your breath hang in the air,
let the clouds thicken,
let the sky sink.

Let winter come.

A LIFE ASCENDING

(A reflection on dying, death and bereavement)

℅

JOHN HUNT

The day before, they asked for confirmation that he was dying, and I gave it.

Now, entering the room where his body lay and his partner sat weeping quietly, it was the music, 'The Lark Ascending', the violin carrying the melody, soaring, singing, up and up, that stirred the emotion in me.

It was the quiet death room, a room in a house where he had known that he would die, and had said so, and had surrendered to it, as one being overwhelmed by disease and embraced by death.

He was loved, and in many ways that had been why I had felt so drawn to help and so drawn to 'be there' and to share and support and listen and cry with him; his partner and his family. He was a central figure in a large family of personalities, partners and children, and they were around him and had their individual and collective time with him, and he lived in frailty and was loved.

They had married, he and his partner, knowing that he was ill, but wanting to cement in that civil partnership, their love for each other. Both partners were creative and their circle of friends was large and artistic and they were loved and warmed and supported by it.

In his final months an urge to visit his home county had led to an enquiry to the hospice about support from his partner and my meeting with them and his twin. His partner and his brother had given up their working lives to care for him, because he was loved. A sudden, and significant deterioration, had determined that he would stay in and around his home patch, and his partner, with great ingenuity and strength, organised home rental for a week, or weeks. We, the hospice, organised a succession of moves, taking bed, oxygen, chair, wheelchair, and him, to and fro, up and downstairs and settling him into another house or flat. He knew them all; this was his home turf, close by the sea. He wanted to look out over the sea and sand, where his childhood had been lived, active and inexhaustible and where he was loved.

It was rare to have time alone with him, but finding that opportunity he was unguarded and spoke about dying and was fearful and tearful and, as any young man would, wanted to live, but knew that his time was limited. He had an inner strength, borne of the ability to live in the moment and appreciate what was then, and to know that he was loved.

His body changed; a swollen limb, an increasing weakness and dependence on others to move position and to do the simplest tasks. Nevertheless, he was always welcoming, even when he might not stay awake for long and his frailty of body began to be matched by his frailty of mind.

His partner, whom I admired more with each meeting, learnt to manage oxygen cylinders and a host of other caring skills. Naturally compassionate, he was also considerate towards the needs of the family, particularly the twin. He gave them time at the bedside, but was never far away and never wanted to be, because he loved.

At the final move, a most extraordinary experience; his partner, twin and I, lifting him in a wheelchair over the step and into the hallway and spontaneously, all three of them, bursting into song, and he, matching their strength of voice briefly and, all three enjoying the moment, a memory to store for those that would remain, a brief moment of joy for him. The outlook, in the room where he would die, was onto a garden and, in the warm air, the windows could be wide open and scents and sounds float in and around. It was the oldest of the temporary 'homes' in this lived experience and seemed somehow fitting as an endpoint for him. He knew it, of course, this was his home turf, where, with his brothers and sisters he had spent idyllic summers, memories that now served him well; it was where he was loved.

And so he died there; he knew that he would and had said so. In the immediate time afterwards, there was much practical activity. For us, the hospice, what had become his mobile facility of equipment was gathered in, cleaned and returned to storage, neat and tidy until required again, because that was its purpose.

His funeral, back in the city where he and his partner had made their home was the most incredible affair. The crematorium hall was full to overflowing, people sat on the floor and in the aisles. One of his brothers, glorious in his full military uniform, urged more people in to find a space, 'he loved everyone here'. His partner spoke through tears, of a love and a loss; a friend read a poem; the humanist leader of the ceremony spoke about the privilege of having been able to meet the person that she was speaking about, and how he had wanted to meet her; because he knew what was to come; and there was music, 'The Lark Ascending' filling the hall and one felt the surge of love for his departing, a life ascending.

I felt the need to be at the funeral and to say my own goodbye. There were flowers, roses, but for the congregation to take away, in remembrance of one who was loved.

Time has passed since this experience and my long time in hospice service moves onward. In any interaction with a patient, one hopes to be attentive, empathetic and professional. And yet, on reflection, it is difficult to explain why certain people and families touch one so deeply. Perhaps, there is a fatality; a conjunction of circumstances which deem that this meeting will occur. I was not the only person from my service to be touched by these individuals, this couple, this family group and this episode of care. Others contributed greatly in a range of ways and, our own teamwork and flexibility was undoubtedly enabling, as our patient and his family lived their nomadic lifestyle to support his wish to live until he died in the place that he had been born and grown in. But it was in the relationships and in the 'being there' and 'watching with' that one felt the privilege of our work, and for me, it was the love, the mark of a life lived joyfully with partner, family and friends, that shone through this experience. Not unique, but special in my vocational life, and I am a better person, and grateful for being able to journey some of the way with him and them all.

POLLY DOLLY

ം

MAUREEN GALLAGHER

Monday. Your first day on the rota; your week to come to a conclusion. You have the casting vote.

Sarah sits in her armchair in the sitting room, eyes closed. Saying her prayers. You slip quietly out to the kitchen to cook the dinner. Uninterrupted. But Sarah is on red alert. The first sound of a lid on a pot and out she bullets. 'Mother, its okay,' you say, 'everything's prepared, you can rest while I get on with it.' To no avail. Sarah positions herself at the sink. Washing and re-washing plates. Preparing Rufus' nth meal for the day. Tidying up. And there you are, trying to stretch around her for a colander, to wash a spoon, to get a dishcloth. The kitchen's a warzone.

She *can* do things. Preparing vegetables she can certainly do. Or making pancakes. Take making pancakes. On Wednesday morning she's inside recovering from a restless night and you decide to make pancakes for breakfast. You prepare the batter and leave it in the fridge to settle. Down for a shower, mouth salivating at the thought of freshly-made pancakes. You wash and dry the hair, nice and leisurely. Then up to the kitchen. The smell hits you as soon as you open the door. 'Your pancakes are done,' says Sarah, beaming. And there they are! The pancakes. Stacked high in the oven. All rubbery and hardening by the minute.

There's the confusion.

'I'll go home now,' she'll say. At least once a day.

'You *are* at home.'

'No, I'm not! What are you talking about?'

She looks at you with an expression of both puzzlement and bemusement.

'Mother, you've lived here for 60 years. This is your home.'

'Is it?'

She stands in the middle of the floor, looking around. 'It doesn't seem like my home.'

'Whose home do you think it is?'

'It's your home.'

'No, it's yours,' I say.

'Is it really?' She looks around again. 'Gosh, isn't it looking lovely.'

'You did a great job,' you say.

'And where do you live?'

'I live in London.'

'You live in London.'

'Yes. You've been to my house, you probably don't remember. You were over for my 50th birthday.'

'Oh, the memory I have.'

'Don't worry. You've enough people around to remind you of things.'

'So you live in London?'

'I live in London.'

'I must come over and visit you in London sometime.'

She's 89, going on 90.

Then there's Rufus. Her little dog. Sarah loves Rufus. And why wouldn't she? He trails after her everywhere. Where she goes, he goes. A doll of a dog. Champagne-coloured with two brown marbles for eyes. 'He's the cleanest dog,' Sarah'll say.

Rufus pees regularly in the hall. The bathroom. The kitchen occasionally, for a bit of variety. When Sarah sees a mess, she rushes to clean up. 'Rufus never does this,' she'll insist, scrubbing furiously. You keep your own counsel.

'He's the cleanest little dog. I don't know what got into him. Must be something he ate.'

So Rufus, guilty as sin, pees everywhere, just as the mood takes him. What's not to like about this dog? Not to mention when you lie down on the only comfortable seat – aside from Sarah's armchair – both the dog and Sarah get annoyed. For doesn't Rufus always lie on the back of this sofa, exactly where you want to put your accursed head? Rufus growls and Sarah consoles him. You hate dogs!

The microwave. There's a ban on wet dog food, so Sarah has taken to putting the dry dog food into the microwave: 'The poor wee fellow, he hasn't had a thing to eat today,' she'll say. This will be his tenth meal of the day! Rufus is a smart dog. If he ate all he was given he wouldn't fit in the door. She mixes in with the dog biscuits anything she can find in the fridge – yoghurt, cheese, plum pudding. The meat for the dinner, too, if you don't watch.

So you hide things. Or throw them out. You get rid of all soft foods that might end up in the microwave. Take to hiding the meat up on the very top shelf of the fridge away at the back, just in case. With a tub of vegetable spread towards the front as camouflage. But this woman is on a mission. And her mission field is the kitchen.

☙

Thursday. Morning. Sarah is in her chair in the front room, saying her prayers, by all appearances dead to the world. You nip out to do an errand. You've only gone as far as the car, when you realise you've forgotten your keys. You open the back door and there she is! Going like the clappers – she doesn't hear you on account of not having her hearing aid in – banging around the kitchen, fridge door open, saucepans out, vegetables, working flat out to get the dinner ready. At eleven o'clock in the morning! She's been waiting for you to leave the house. Now she stands, triumphant, with the vegetables prepared, PLUS the steak you'd so carefully hidden, out on the board chopped in half and ready to grill. Six whole hours of vigilance to ensure that the sirloin doesn't end up in the pesky mutt's dish!

She lifts things and puts them away.

'Mother,' you say to her Thursday evening, having searched, 'the cream for the pudding seems to have disappeared. I was certain we had the most of a carton left…'

Sarah takes hold of your elbow, looks you straight in the eye and says *sotto voce*, 'I don't like to say this, but that Claire takes things from me, stuff for her own dog…that's likely where the cream went.'

'Mother, I'm Claire.'

'Oh.' Flustered, 'I didn't mean you…'

'Plus, I've no dog.' You close the fridge door firmly, loosening her elbow clinch. You have to have the last word on this one. You find the cream in a bowl in the hot press later.

❦

Friday. Five o'clock on the button, as soon as she hears the musical sound of a saucepan, out Sarah charges. Takes up position at the sink, as per usual. Elbows out. Ready for battle.

'Mother,' you say, 'why don't you go into the sitting room and have a rest, you've already prepared the vegetables?' You lift the lids one by one to show her.

'I want to help.'

'You can do the dishes after.'

'Okay, so. My back is killing me.'

She wants to sit down? So why is she out in the kitchen annoying you? What is she trying to prove?

You heat the plates. Serve the food. Call Sarah. Sarah has just settled into her seat when she notices Rufus, looking at them with his two big brown marbles. Up she jumps. 'I must get something for Rufus, the poor wee thing, he hasn't eaten all day.' She hurries about, moving as fast as joints allow. She pours some nuts into the dog dish, then cuts up some of her own meat and potato to mix in with his food. Swishes the whole mélange around with her hand. You do some deep breathing.

It's not easy to have a conversation with Sarah.

'How are the children?' she asks.

'They're good. Rebecca is in Paris.'

'Mnn?' She can't hear without the hearing aid. You have to say everything twice.

'Rebecca is in Paris,' you shout. Talking is a strain.

'The weather is dry, that's a good thing.' Sarah wants a conversation. 'And how are the family?'

'They're good. Rebecca is in Paris.' You make the effort. 'She's teaching English.'

Afterwards Sarah spoons out the pudding, giving you the larger portion.

She insists on doing the wash-up by herself, tells you to go in and sit down.

You ring Blathnaid.

'So how's mother?'

'Oh, you know...the kitchen! Plus, she won't wear her hearing aid.'

'She says it whistles in her ear.'

So hard to have a conversation. You keep your voice low. 'She asked me yesterday if I was related to her.' You've visited the new home in Carrick. Very clean. Lovely staff. You have to make a decision soon.

Sarah is suddenly in the room with a hot water bottle. She returns to the kitchen closing the door behind her. Could she have been listening?

'She's just brought me in a water bottle, for my knees?'

'She won't wear the long johns I bought her, says they're for old people.'

Without warning, the sitting room door snaps open and Sarah is back in the room again.

'Would you like a cup of tea?'

You say, 'no thanks', but Sarah doesn't move.

'Who are you talking to?'

'Blathnaid…she's coming back tomorrow.'

'What were ye talking about?'

Is she aware of the Damocles sword over her head?

That evening you both settle into the sitting room, you with your book, head resting on Rufus's favourite spot. Sarah with her beads. But tonight, she doesn't pray.

You reflect on your life back in London, longing to be back. To your ballroom dancing, meeting up with friends. You're here less than a week, and already you're suffering from cabin fever. You have to come to a conclusion soon.

You glance at Sarah. She's sitting there, newspaper on her lap; looking into the middle distance, drumming her fingers on the arm of the chair as if deep in thought. As if planning tomorrows trip to town or a visit to a friend, or some problem she must solve, some plant she must buy. But she'll do none of those things.

You turn on the telly.

'Can you turn it up,' Sarah asks. You turn it up. She never usually watches TV. It's very uncomfortable to have to listen to the TV at full volume. You surreptitiously turn it down a little.

'Would you mind turning it up a little more?' Sarah asks almost immediately.

At the ad break, she says: 'Where is that happening?'

'India and Thailand.'

'Isn't it sad for those people?'

'Very sad.' And then you both talk about the tsunami – or rather you talk and Sarah sits engrossed, delighted to be having a conversation. To be connected.

Sarah spreads the sheepskin cloth over her knees, lifts Rufus up onto her lap and strokes him. You bring up the old days. How Sarah met your father. How, when he was at college, Sarah went to work at the Polly Dolly factory, the money was needed. You've heard it all before.

'I hated working there.'

You know that. The other girls there – town girls – were coarse, foul mouthed.

'It's not that I was a snob. Just that the other girls, well, they were very rough.'

You say nothing.

'There was one nice girl there, I made friends with.'

Maria was her name.

'Maria was her name. I liked Maria but I hated being there.'

Yes, because the other girls were the wrong sort.

'The manager used to call us his Polly Dollies. Maria said he had a thing for me.'

Wait a minute! This was new. You've not heard this before.

'He paid me a lot of attention. Always showing me how to do things.'

Your heart skips a beat. A middle-aged manager showing a pretty country girl extra attention?

'Then, one day he asked me to come into his office. To help with filing, he said. There'd be extra money.'

You're holding your breath.

'He tried to kiss me, the dirty blackguard.'

A married manager sets his sights on one of his workers. A teenager. Oh, my God!

'He was stroking my hair, hands all over me. He kept on trying to kiss me but I wouldn't let him. The rascal.'

All the while she's talking, her face is flushed. It's as if she's back there. Defying this manager who had his eyes fixed on one of his Polly Dollies.

'I hated the place. In the end I just said I was leaving. And I left.'

For the first time in your life, you consider the possibility that your mother's life could have taken a different path. That you might never have been born.

☙

Saturday. Morning. Sarah is in fine form, having slept well.

'Look at the daffodils,' Sarah says, looking out the window at the miniatures in the window box, 'aren't they lovely.'

'It's spring. I love spring.' You feel good. Only one more day.

'Isn't it wonderful too, how they come up every year. You know, they die down and then the next thing up they pop again a year later. Year after year.'

'Yes, it is amazing.'

'How is it that they come up again every year? How does it happen?'

She is looking at you wide-eyed, waiting to be brought into the natural world, the essences of things. She has her hearing aid in. You talk to her about first beginnings, the big bang, the evolution of life. And suddenly you're back talking to your own children when they were small.

'Some say that all there was at the beginning was a tiny point, that built up so much energy it exploded. It exploded and everything that is in this world was shot out from that tiny point of singularity. This planet was made up of fragments from that explosion. But at first there was no life. Only water and storm. Gradually the water subsided. And during one particularly bad storm life emerged. At first there were only fishes.'

Sarah looks at you with the openness of a child, as you unfold the heretical tale of the evolution of plants, animals and man. Listening to the words. Feeling the excitement in your voice. Overjoyed to be part of a conversation. To be engaged. Involved.

'Then, there were lizards, then dinosaurs, then primates. And then us. And along the way, all along the way, plants.'

'It's amazing the way they come up every year the same as before,' Sarah says. Here's a woman who can't remember what she did five minutes ago and yet she's full of wonder about life on earth.

'Plants, like us need light and food. They grow from a tiny seed and like us they die. The plant that comes up this year is related to, but not the same as, the one last year.'

'I'm nearly 90,' says Sarah, 'I can't believe I've lasted this long.'

'You're a great age.'

'My memory isn't good but apart from that I've a good life.'

'You have.'

'I'm not ready to throw in the towel yet,' she says.

'And why would you?' you say.

As you drive through the lush Tipperary countryside en route to the airport and home, the sun is beaming; everything appears fresh and bright and brimful of life. No need to make a decision yet.

A MATTER OF COMPASSION

ɞ

ALVA DE CHIRO

It's a funny time six o'clock in the morning, not quite day time. The dawn chorus is chirping and next door's white cat pads down the path. Hunting time over, till darkness returns. I caress my warm mug, and savour the first sip of tea. One of the pleasures of life. Then I begin to think. It's a ritual. I go over everything. Everyone I run into say it's therapeutic. I hope so, because widowhood is a new status for me. My thinking always begins in the same way, with the words...

'Mr Johnson the x-ray has shown a mass in your chest.' Hard to take in. We thank the chest physician and say goodbye. Further appointments are to be arranged and a different life begins. A life of hospitals, menus of nutritious drinks, to wash down numerous tablets. Tablets for sickness and for pain. Chats about holidays and days out are no longer on the agenda. Friends who visit don't really know what to say, they feel uncomfortable visiting a terminally ill man, because it's painful to see the golfer, gardener, traveller, so reduced in size. Not that Rob behaves any differently, there's still a joke and a wry remark. In fact I've noticed in the palliative care clinic an air of camaraderie, all the patients are courageous. Sometimes I have to reprimand myself and mutter, 'Annette Johnson, a miserable face won't help Rob, he needs to know you are coping.' I remember when we came back from the hospital, with a devastating prognosis. I was crying and wanted to sit looking into space, but Rob said, 'Let's have a cuppa and a run

71

out into the countryside.' He couldn't bear to have me crying over him. And he was right.

Outside it's getting lighter, looks as though it might be sunny. I'll probably be able to get into the garden later. Gardening is therapeutic.

Hospices have wonderful gardens. Our hospice is surrounded by beautiful grounds with velvety lawns and colourful flower beds. Seats in memory of loved ones are placed in summer houses and between leafy trees. It is lovely. I really don't know what my husband's thoughts are as I wheel him along the paths. I can only imagine. Was he wishing that he could have been allowed a few more years to spend with his family and his grandchildren. Had he any unfulfilled ambitions. Was he hoping for a peaceful death. I don't know. But what I did know was that he had asked me, our GP and the consultant to help him die.

A car speeds down the avenue, it's the young lad from the end bungalow. He'll be late for work as usual. Yes Rob wanted to die. Easily, peacefully and with dignity. When you can't breathe fresh air, get soil under your nails, eat a tasty meal with the family, give your grandkids a cuddle. And can make no plans for tomorrow, then what is there to live for?

I can feel myself getting all worked up. The paper boy's coming up the path. Rob'd always have a chat with him about football. But Rob had to suffer. Then as if I'm in parliament, I begin my rehearsed speech. I'm addressing the dog, the cushions and the furniture. My words flow with passion: 'If you can't breathe, speak, digest, swallow, urinate, excrete and have become so thin that to move is impossible, then in this country that is it! When are you lot going to get some sense and put an end to unnecessary and unbearable suffering? Why have folks to travel to Switzerland, when they want to die at home? Why did my Rob have to endure a horrible death, choking on his own saliva, with me at his side? All the care of the hospice staff could not prevent it. So is that what you'd like to watch?' The dog's looking at me as if I'm mad!

My tea's cold, better make another one, with a couple of slices of toast and marmalade. Everybody says: 'Don't neglect yourself. Rob wouldn't want you to.' But now I've got a purpose. I hope it will help to fill the Rob-shaped hole that fills my inside and which makes me feel so lonely. I've become an onlooker. The world goes on. The couple across the road set off in their car, going shopping or for a meal at a country inn. Now I think they look so smug and I feel like shouting: 'Your turn will come.' Isn't that horrible? But that's how I feel. This world is made for twos, and no one can imagine what it is like to lose your soulmate, unless it has happened to you. My friend who is a widow has helped me a lot by just listening, and letting me cry for as long as I needed. Tears embarrass some folks and they keep away as if you've got a highly infectious disease. If you can't cry when you lose your husband, when can you? That's what I think anyway. I've discovered that distraction is wonderful, even if it stops you going over the illness and death, just for half-an-hour. I think eventually I'll join some classes. I used to enjoy writing short stories and botanical drawing so I'll find out about those.

My great crusade is going to be fighting for the laws of this country to be changed. Dignity in dying that's my motto, it's a matter of compassion.

ENHANCING DEMENTIA RECIPE

ᘒ

JANET WILLOUGHBY

Ingredients

1 resident

1 ambulance with trimmings

Bright lights

1 kilo noise

1 emergency room

2 junior doctors

1 registrar

Several nurses

Hypodermic needles

Venflon

X-ray

1 porter

A large helping of pain and difficulty expressing wishes

0 Advance Statement or Decision

Method

Remove the resident from familiar surroundings. Carefully place on cold, hard trolley (trolley best left to chill in night air).

If you have distressed family members, whisk them in at this point.

Wrap resident in hypothermic foil bag, season with tight straps and shake well.

When you are happy that the seasoning is well distributed, leave to marinate in ambulance: this shouldn't take long. Add banging doors and sirens for extra flavour.

In due course remove resident from ambulance and examine with two junior doctors plus registrar if you have one available. Several nurses should be added at this point, change them regularly. Stab resident with hypodermic needles, don't worry if you cannot get the venflon in, you can always try again…and again. X-ray for good measure. Ensure copious mumbling and conversations that are not including the resident.

Add porter, strong flavoured, full of stories and good cheer to transport the resident to a brightly lit busy ward. Make sure that the resident knows nobody, add more nurses. Mix well without listening or understanding, you may need to add sedation at this point.

Pour into a bed, it should be a good confused consistency by now.

Cook in hot ward.

Serve with the need to find a specialist dementia unit.

THE PATIENT THAT CHANGED ME

ℰℑ

FAYE GISHEN

I knocked on the front door and waited anxiously for her husband to answer. His handshake was warm and sincere. He invited me in and I sidestepped the little girl and her puzzles, set up in the hall. He was palpably grateful that help had arrived.

I ventured upstairs, following him into their bedroom; such a personal and private place. It was warm and bright, and she sat at her computer, typing intently.

'Hello,' I offered.

'Hello, how nice of you to come,' she said, no hint of fear or irony, and putting me at ease.

He stayed in the room as we went over the history that I had already heard from others. The cancer was very advanced – her liver was distended, causing her discomfort. Her lungs were involved too, with a fine mesh of malignant cells weaving along the tracks and routes, normally reserved for air and laughter. I warmed to her poetic commentary of the birth and early years of their small daughter, and her heartbreak at no longer being able to contemplate that yearned-for second child. All spoken with fluidity and no hint of malice – and I said nothing, simply listened.

Afterwards I examined her on her bed. Her belly was swollen and hard. The irony that anyone who saw her would think her in the advanced stages of pregnancy, crossed my mind. It was tempting to suggest subjecting her to a scan and possibly draining off some of the cancerous fluid, but intuition told me at this stage, to interfere with her as little as possible. The transient benefits would be outweighed by putting her through yet another procedure. She had made it clear that she wished to remain in the security of her home with her husband, daughter and all familiar things around her. I felt the weight of decision making heavily around me. This is what we are paid to do – make judgements and take difficult decisions. Take the emotion out, I warned myself – forget that she is similar to me – and make a balanced judgement. This is my role. This is the art of being a physician.

It wasn't supposed to have happened like this. Not on any level. I can't say we were friends, but she and I had met, more than once, through a mutual friend, and in my mind this was sufficient for the warning signs to flicker. Many doctors I know wouldn't think twice about treating a friend; in fact some would welcome the opportunity to look after a colleague or acquaintance. I have never enjoyed this privilege. Call it cowardice on my part, or draw any conclusions that you will about me.

Of course, she could be me. I could be me in this vulnerable, surreal and painful situation, with only weeks of life remaining. It could be me, forced to write cards to be given to my daughter at significant events in her future. It could be my hands wrapping the Christmas gift for her husband, lovingly picked out months in advance. It could be me finishing letters to my parents, saved on to the desktop of the computer, for when they are needed. Me, writing instructions for my husband about ballet classes and packed lunches and play dates. Me, trying to organise and control the future in a world full of uncontrollable futures.

And so it continued. Phone calls and visits – with each one came a fresh opening into the future, and a chance to talk through topics that would have seemed inconceivable to discuss only a few months before. A familiarity and trust developing and binding together the patient and doctor. With each visit her hopes, fears and dreams unfolded and were dutifully chronicled. Her reassurances to her parents, who she knew would be broken, that she had had a lovely life and was grateful for everything. Her aspirations for her child and inexplicable sadness that she wouldn't witness her growing; her hopes for her husband – to move on, to be happy again – tinged at the same time with a silent fear that he may be happy again too quickly... Always self-assured and selfless, rarely faltering and only occasionally crying, and betraying her fear.

Gradually, her face became thinner; her zygomatic arches becoming pronounced and impossible to ignore. The fading body but active, keen mind – still with work to do and things to achieve. As her abdomen grew bigger and her liver more distended, she asked for stronger painkillers. I needed to coerce her to take them initially, as she feared developing a brain more clouded than it had been with the chemotherapy.

Then, as time passed, she began to change gear. As her body declined, she started to retreat into herself, her world folding inwards like a concertina, stripping aside the superfluous and leaving only the core. Her husband accepted help on a daily basis now. I think he hoped to revert to being her husband, not her carer, although hopes of physical intimacy had long passed. Strangers invaded their home; initially to help bathe and dress her and after, to set up the syringe pump that whirred through the day and night, administering doses of increasingly necessary painkillers.

Then, one night in the small hours, he called my phone to tell me that she had died in their bed. He was lying next to her with their child between them. Their daughter was asleep and oblivious to the enormity of what had happened. She fell asleep with a mother and father and awoke the next day with only one parent. Their world was irreparably changed. And in a smaller, less significant way, so was mine.

REGRETS

❦

HOPE UCHIO

"I guess I have no choice." This is what you said as you sat there with tears streaming down your face. What had become of you? You used to have rosy cheeks; you used to be plumper. What I saw was a thin body bent over, a hollow face. I saw someone who subsisted on protein drinks and called it "eating." Don't you think I knew? How rough taking care of Dad had been? Yet you sat there looking at me with those pleading eyes. "Don't take him away from me. He's all I've got. He's my life." These are the words I heard in the few moments of silence that enveloped us. They were aimed right at my heart, those words. But I took Dad away from you anyway.

You were past 80 after all; how could you possibly think clearly about your future or even Dad's? I said you needed to rest and regain your strength. You needed to eat well again. My arguments were sound, I thought. Yet my self-interest was all too clear. I was stressed out; my life was being ruined, I said. I couldn't, didn't want to take care of the both of you, I said. And I kept harassing you until you were too exhausted to put up a fight. So when the day came to put Dad into a nursing home, your tears flowed and I refused to change my mind.

I never stopped to consider what this separation might do to you and Dad. You were so distraught; he was all you could think about. You spent your days visiting him and lying in bed at night praying for him. Bedridden and helpless, Dad spent most of his time, alone, in a cold room. He lost weight and endured needless pain in the hands of young, inexperienced caretakers. Dad's Alzheimer's was too far gone. Yet you sensed his suffering, understood his thoughts.

Frequently embroiled in confrontations with the nursing staff over Dad's care, I found no respite, no peace. I didn't stop to consider what love, commitment, respect and dignity really meant.

Six months later, when Dad's condition worsened in the nursing home, I realized it had all been a mistake. Your words, your sadness came back to me with an overwhelming force. So I brought Dad back home to you. And you were both so happy but by then Dad didn't have too much longer to live.

I remember when Dad's body started to give out; he could no longer swallow food properly, so he was taken to the hospital. The doctor said, "It doesn't look good," but I refused to listen. I said, "Mom, I'm going to take a vacation." You nodded your head, looking at me sadly. You wanted me to stay and be strong. You needed me. But I ran away while Dad lay in a hospital bed, unable to eat, his body slowly wasting away. "I'll be back soon," I said, ignoring the voice that said, "Stay!" ignoring your terror and loneliness. By the time I got back, he was already dead.

When Dad died, the shock of his death was too much for you. You had a big fall and cracked your ribs. You were not even able attend his funeral. "Mom, I'm taking you home for a few weeks until you get better," I said. So I took you to my home, bathed you, cooked your meals and spent time with you. I wanted to keep you with me forever. But after the two weeks were up I took you back to that cold, empty house. The night I took you home you came outside to close the gate, saying you would be okay. Then with a heavy heart, I left you. The tears flowed as I sped home in my car. A single thought entered my mind, "Call Mom," but I did not. Instead, I kept driving full speed ahead. That night you had a terrible fall when you went back into the house. You spent the night on the floor in a pool of your urine until someone found you the next morning.

I was drowning in misery every weekend I saw you. My "Hi, Moms" sounded downright cold. You were always so happy to see me. Why was I not happy to see you? Despite the stays in the hospital and the daily visits from home-helpers, you had wanted to live in your own house. And I had agreed to become your weekend caretaker. But as the months went by, I became increasingly irritable and sullen. There were tasks to complete: the washing, cooking, shopping, and the taking care of you. I couldn't see the simple joy of being with you. Yet you always forgave me when I lost my temper. You always said you loved me, knowing that another week of silence and loneliness lay ahead.

"Don't go. Please don't go." I remember those words you said. Your expression was so dark and your eyes had a look of despair. We had surprised you by paying a visit and taking you out for cake and coffee. I had said, "Okay, Mom, so I'll be back in a few days" when we brought you back home. And then you had said those words. But we left you, got in the car and drove off and in my head I heard those words, "Don't go. Please don't go. Don't leave me here all alone." I felt your sadness and loneliness rushing over me like a wave. "Should we go back?" I said to my husband. "No, she'll be all right," he said. Why is it that even now I can still feel that deep pain?

I remember when I said, "They are saying things behind my back, Mom. I can't take it anymore." My relationship with the staff at the small nursing home was deteriorating. They were short-staffed; they needed my help; and so I helped, reluctantly. Oh, yes, I thought I suffered. But you were the one who was bedridden and suffering from mild dementia. You were the one who was constantly confused and anxious because of short-term memory loss. You were the one who had to depend on the staff for every little thing. Who was the one who couldn't take it anymore? Did I ever stop to think of that?

I remember standing by your bed with M. and P. in the hospital room, watching you breathe heavily into your oxygen mask. You gripped my hand tightly and held on to it when I tried to let it go. You had a terrified look on your face. I knew what you were trying to say: "I'm all alone. Please don't leave me here all alone." You held on to my hand with all your might. But I let go of your hand, giving into my own need for sleep and rest. The next morning the nurse said you had stayed awake all night. I knew you were afraid of being alone; afraid of falling asleep; afraid of dying. But I still let go of your hand.

I remember you were breathing hard. "Is it new?" you whispered, looking at my shirt and smiling. "No," I said. I stood by your bed looking at you. You motioned me with your hand to come to the other side of the bed. Then you looked up and said, "I love you," and I leaned down close to your face and said, "I love you, too." You pursed your lips to kiss me. I hesitated and kissed you on the forehead. I didn't know then that was my last chance to kiss you, your last chance to show me your love.

At your funeral, they said to me, "You were always there for her; you always took care of your mom; you were her treasure." Yes, I want to pat myself on the back; I want to congratulate myself. Oh, how I want to take comfort in the fact that I took care of you, that I was a good daughter. That is what I cannot do.

Your deep faith in God: that is what really sustained you. Spending most of your lives as missionaries in Japan, you and Dad learned to trust and rely on God in all circumstances. God comforted you. But human beings fall short. I fell short.

My mean words; unkind deeds; neglect; hesitation; and insensitivity, that is what keeps coming back to me. I cannot undo, cannot take back those things I did and said to you. I cannot bring you back and say, "Let me make it up to you." I cannot say "I am sorry" because "I am sorry" will never reach you.

A DOSE OF REALITY

ᏣᎳ

CAROLINE SPOSTO

My sister Rosemary lay dying. For three days, this reality had hung over us without entirely sinking in. Her hospital room had the atmosphere of a casual open house; warm greetings, comings and goings of close friends and family. She drifted in and out of sleep amid a chaos of tubes and machinery. Though shockingly bloated and more jaundiced than words can describe, her clear voice and flawless smile hadn't changed since she had competed in local beauty pageants decades before.

Rosemary's liver had failed. So had the doctors' attempts to heal it. In her case, a transplant wasn't an option. She fought on valiantly—brightening at the sight of familiar faces, complimenting my necklace, asking for spoonfuls of ice chips, not once forgetting to say the "*please*" and "*thank you*" our mother instilled in the five of us when we were small. Throughout those blurred days, various medical professionals made the rounds in and out of her hospital room.

One afternoon, a less familiar doctor came in with the latest lab reports. All of the chairs around Rosemary's bed were occupied by well-wishers. She had just woken up. My brother-in-law greeted the doctor and casually asked her how things were going. She looked up from the chart, glanced at us as if she were taking the temperature of the ambiance in the room, and then said, point blank—*ostensibly to my sister's husband, but actually to everyone present*—that Rosemary wasn't expected to live.

We felt as if we had been doused with ice water. When we managed to catch our breath, all eyes were then on my sister staring silently at the doctor. We never saw Rosemary smile or heard her speak again.

The doctor made an officious exit as we struggled for equilibrium in the wake of her words. I managed to collect myself and follow her down the corridor. When I caught up with her, I demanded, "*Why did you do that?*"

"Because, you needed to know," she said, matter-of-factly; stopping only because I blocked her path.

"We *did* know," I said. "We were keeping our spirits up for *her* sake."

When I got back to the room, the damage was palpable. The doctor's words had instantly cast my sister into an emotional abyss. Our strong, supportive team was now a pathetic group of helpless bystanders. Rosemary looked through us with sad, terrified eyes and 48 hours later, she was gone. Although my sister had been in a condition that made her death imminent, her final hours on earth weren't ruined by liver failure. They were ruined by a poisonous *dose of reality*.

My brother-in-law hadn't asked "How's it going?" with the intention of forcing a crisis. My sister had been conscious and lucid. *She hadn't asked whether or not she was going to die.* It was as if that doctor found the calm, uplifting atmosphere troubling in light of my sister's condition and she was duty bound to deliver a heavy dose of reality. My brother-in-law's innocuous question made an easy target for her verbal bomb. In short, the doctor had assumed that we were in denial.

In today's culture of candidness, that word: "*denial*" has been elevated from buzzword to cardinal sin. Anyone who has ever been privy to an over-talkative coffee klatch or girls' night out knows how eager we have become to sew a scarlet "*D*" on anyone who demurs from a game of "Verbal Strip Poker" to lay bare a difficult personal situation.

Contrary to the doctor's assessment, our family was not in denial. We had done our homework. We understood the magnitude of the crisis. Rosemary had been a lawyer, a real estate broker, and an accomplished horsewoman. She had adopted a surly Rottweiller whose previous owner considered dangerously undisciplined and trained him into an obedient pet. She was no wimp. When she felt she was up to the truth, she would have asked for it. At that point, her attitude would have been, "Give it to me straight, I can take it." Forcing the dose of reality on her before she had the strength to bear it seemed every bit as cruel as forcing a patient with a broken leg to run a marathon.

We parrot a lot of truisms on the subject of *truth*. Our culture places a high value on it—varnished or unvarnished—our business or none of our business—we treat it like gold. When it comes to ethics, personal integrity, and fair-and-square dealing, "the truth, the whole truth and nothing but the truth" should be our 24-carate gold standard. But when we are determined to pull back the curtain at any time, in any place or situation, ethical questions arise.

In recent years, with the help of technology, our over-communicative tendencies have crowded out the breathing room that once allowed other human beings the sanctity of an inner life and the dignity of private pain. Google-search sensibilities have given us the liberty and license to probe, stalk and fact-check people and information that were once respected and left alone. Somewhere along this road, we developed an appetite for truths that were particularly unvarnished and rough: deliberately unflattering paparazzi shots of movie stars without makeup, embarrassing arguments on reality television, and worse. We think nothing of indulging our impulses to act as amateur investigators, self-appointed judges and self-styled critics; staring when we should avert our eyes, probing when we should curb our curiosity and commenting when we should be silent—*all in the sacred name of truth*. Where ethics go, philosophy follows and this begs the question: What is truth, and does a factual accounting always provide it?

The truth did not set my sister free. It did the opposite. The wisdom that even an ideal as pure as truth has certain limitations still prevails in other parts of the world. When my great-grandmother arrived in the United States a little before the turn of the twentieth century, that idea still prevailed here.

Everyone in my family grew up hearing the story that our great-grandmother had been orphaned as a child in "the old country." She was then adopted by a wealthy family and grew up in a mansion with servants. She had a genteel life, but when she was 17 years old, a sense of adventure set her against her adoptive parents' wishes and she abandoned her lavish surroundings to travel to Colorado as a mail order bride. The moment she saw my great-grandfather—the stranger in the train station who three days later, was to become her husband—she was smitten by his good looks and fell instantly in love. She and her husband raised 12 children on a small farm. Those children faced the same challenges and hardships as other immigrant's children of that time, but their mother's story about her daring decision set them apart with an extra boost of courage and dignity. Three generations later, I continued to move upward supported by the handrail of that tale. It was only in recent years that someone listened with skepticism and then suggested I look into it with the help of a popular genealogical research service. I pondered their suggestion, and ultimately decided not to find out. Suppose that I were to learn that my great-grandmother's "old country" life was full of misfortune and misery instead of privilege and adventure? For the sake of argument, imagine that she had raised her children on that daily dose of reality? Would they have held their heads as high? Done as well in school? Dared to dream as big?

I once had a conversation with a rags-to-riches entrepreneur. I asked him the secret of his success against impossible odds. He reflected for a moment and then said, "Well… I didn't know that it was impossible, and so I just went ahead and did it."

In other words, beating adversity takes a level of energy that can only be sustained by a happy human being. Depriving people of their optimism by telling them something "for their own good" often does them no good at all.

Don't get me wrong. I do value honesty. I would never advocate leaving difficult historical truths about social injustices whitewashed "for the public good." I'm not suggesting we accept deviousness, evasiveness and outright lies about matters that concern us. I'm not in support of inflated compliments and gratuitous flattery as a means of raising anyone's self-esteem.

But some truths are more necessary than others, and contrary to current trends, we do not have the right—let alone the moral imperative—to intrude on someone else's inner world for the mere sake of deflating the notion that keeps them afloat in rough water. In today's tell-all world, each of us bears a greater responsibility to ignore the crowd, to exercise our best judgment in matters of discretion, to contain our curiosity and consider our words before we give them a life of their own.

I once advised my daughters that there are two kinds of people: the kind of people that others are always happy to see, and the kind others are not always happy to see. In most cases the "truth at all costs" people fall into that second category.

It was difficult to relive my sister's death in sufficient detail to write about it, but if someone reads this essay and then thinks twice before they deliver a harmful dose of truth, it was worth the effort.

After two and a half years, I still haven't found the grace to forgive the doctor for crushing my sister's spirit, though I managed to forget her name. In that way my anger is on the action and not the person.

Words are powerful things. We are not under oath in every situation. When we feel tempted to give people a dose of reality, we should consider the Hippocratic oath: *First do no harm.*

CLOSING SCENES

ℰↄ

GRÁINNE TOBIN

Delighted yo-hoes from the side ward
as she models the creased and outgrown nightie
her baffled husband sent, the kind of thing men do.

She stumbles in the back door, bloodied as from battle,
holding a gauze pad to the spurting wound
where they botched the shunt, scorched the blistered skin –
and carrying a daughter's Christmas skateboard
bought between hospital and home.

The phone voice says it has never been policy to issue
disabled motorists' parking discs merely on a temporary
basis.
These are reserved for registered drivers
genuinely experiencing impediments to mobility.
What exactly is the nature of this temporary problem?
She grips the mouthpiece, answers: I have advanced cancer.
Connected by pulsing cable,
handsets warmed to common body heat,
each contemplates the meaning of temporary.
Life, a self-limiting condition.

At home where she is put to bed
on vivid linen chosen long ago,
nurses and neighbours pass through muffled doors.
Cradled, she chases sleep, sweats out dark hours
struggling for sense. Beyond the tenderness
of smoothed-out sheets, she labours
towards deliverance, cherished but alone.

On that last night she comes to her friend in a dream,
able to speak and move again, to share
the big hug, the pillowy warmth of skin.
I'm dying, she shrugs, and laughing,
they shake their heads as if to say,
Well, wouldn't you know? Sure isn't that always the way?

Typed-up instructions: keep clergy out of this,
invite a union speaker, hire the community hall.
She wants Bread of Heaven chorused by rugby players,
her coffin's pathway lined with high-stepping Irish dancers,
uilleann pipes for our tears
and later, a fluted reel
to lift us back
out of the dark of her grave.

AN HONOURABLE LIFE

⁂

CHRISTOPHER OWEN

'I don't care,' she heard him say.

There she was in the living room, looking first at him, he with his back to her, and then at the pills scattered over the carpet where they had fallen from his dressing gown. There must have been a whole month's supply. Well, it was downright disgusting. 'If you don't take your pills you'll die!' she said to him.

'I don't care,' he had replied – no more than in a whisper – not turning to face her.

'You want to die?' she asked, irritated.

'I don't care,' she heard him say.

Here was this man, her husband, who had every weekday for 45 years caught the 8.03 to London Bridge Station, had walked across London Bridge to his office in the City, and taken lunch at the Kardoma and later, when Kardomas were no more, at a cafe off Fenchurch Street called The Mitre. Here was this man who returned home to Hither Green every evening on the 5.23. All these years he had been a civil servant, and in the 15 years before retirement had been up there in the top ranks of his profession. He had committed himself to his work, had been proud to have been a public servant. A man of honour, truthful to the last. Fastidious. A man of habit. Every evening he had brought home the *Evening Standard*. Every evening he had enjoyed the dinner she had set before him. Generous to her at all times, private as a person beyond all others she had known. 'I don't care,' she heard him say.

He wanted to die, did he? she asked this gentleman, this kind and courteous father of two boys who'd not, at least in their mother's opinion, come up to expectations, this uncomplaining and patient husband, he with a nervous cough that preceded his arrival, he with his intermittent singing, those snatches of Gilbert and Sullivan, although she had had to rebuke him on occasion when, out of doors, he would break into soft song. 'Poor Wandering One'; 'They stole the Prince and Brought Him Here' – those were his favourites. This was the gentleman who, opening the oven door, had discovered a chicken roasting inside. 'I'm so sorry,' he had said to it – him not wishing to have disturbed it. This man was he, who, in order to ascertain whether or not she or his sons required additional finance, would circumspectly enquire: 'And how is the Chancellor of the Exchequer?'

He faced the wall. The pills all over the carpet. 'I don't care.' she heard him say.

The man had no legs to him now, which was his frequent frustrated complaint.

'My legs,' he complained, 'they won't move.' And hadn't he always enjoyed a good brisk walk, and hadn't he often walked up on Beachy Head with her on their many summer visits to Eastbourne? And that last summer, he had hobbled there on Beachy Head, impatient at his incapacity, and had fallen down as they had begun to return to the promenade. And she had been unable to get him to his feet. Not 'til help had come along. It had been a frustration for her. A terrible embarrassment. For she had never been comfortable with illness. She had set her sights on this young man from North Wales. He was a good catch for he was a professional man – a civil servant with the Inland Revenue. No tradesman, he. She had been a nurse – best years of her life, she was to say – but after she had married him she had gone up in the world, had begun to hobnob with the professional classes. One afternoon all those years ago she had thrown her nursing medals and references to the back of the coal fire, and in that moment had put an end to her past. In her day, she was to say, young ladies did not go to work. She had feared her nursing career would be greeted with disapproval. When she was a small child her father had deserted the family, had gone off with another woman. Her mother as a consequence had found herself near destitute and had been obliged to put her, and her brothers and sister into a children's home where they had remained for nine years. It was a time that, in later years, she was unwilling to recall.

Here was this man then, her husband, whom on their wedding night, countless years ago, she had interrupted as he had stood at the mirror in the bathroom, him wearing his dressing gown and cleaning his teeth. She had entered without knocking and he had politely and shyly asked her if she did not think that, in entering as she had, she had unwittingly exposed herself to a charge, however small, of impropriety. This had been the man who, this past year and more, could not now stand at the toilet and do what he had to do without her help. His hands had become so shaky, his penis, on account, as she assumed, of his illness, so shrivelled, that she was obliged to hold it for him so as to direct it down towards the bowl in order that he didn't splash all over the toilet floor.

Throughout their married life she had made her own clothes. She had decorated and furnished the house, upholstered the chairs, made the curtains, planted out the garden. Learnt French. Took up painting in oils. She was creative. He was proud of her. He often said so. He had become old and frail. He suffered a mild heart attack. One morning she brought him his cup of tea and found blood on his sheets. 'What have you done?' she asked him.

He could not say. The blood had come from his scrotum. He had attempted in the night to get up to go to the lavatory. He had sat up with his legs over the side of the bed and had caught his testicles under him. He had impatiently yanked at them with his fingers to free them. His nails had cut into them. She, that morning of this discovery, had had him lie back on the bed, while she put a sticking plaster over the cut. The following day she found he had done the same thing all over again. She applied fresh sticking plaster. She had no way of hiding her irritation and distress. She hated the indignity. It made her ill. He faced the wall. He had turned his back on his life.

'I don't care,' he said.

They awarded him the CBE in the year he retired. She bought him a gold watch to celebrate. He was so pleased and proud of her gift to him. He had a boyish smile. A boyish smile and a quiet way. Why had he not, she had from time to time complained to him – and later in her life was to complain to her grown-up sons – why had he not taken stronger action with the boys when they had been badly behaved? He had always answered her that he hoped the boys would learn from their example. He believed that the character of a man or woman was with him or her from birth and was fundamentally unchangeable. At the end of life there was death. After death, he had always said, there was nothing more.

He stood facing the wall with his back to her, his secret scattered at his feet, and he declined her rebuke. 'I don't care,' he said.

A week later he was to fall. He was blue in the face. She was unable to get him up. She tried to shove cushions under him to prop him up. The boys should be there, she lamented. She was not well herself. She angrily dialled 999. The ambulance came. As they took him away to the hospital, he kept calling her name. She did not go with him. She remained to tidy the house, to put things away. He died before the night was out.

She rang the boys.

'He said he didn't care,' she told them.

'I don't care,' she heard him say.

And the words pierced her, and she was full with grief.

OF GLASS, OF LIGHT, OF SILVER

cɔ

KIT DE WAAL

Morphine is wonderful. Without the angry distraction of pain, I can catch the wind and fill my sails.

I see you. I see a little boy, sandy skinned, moat-making, concentrating. You squat like a tribal child and scoop a channel to the sea. I see you with sticks and rocks and shells, stamping, war-dancing with the waves, salty gusts in your sticky white curls. I towel you dry and wrap my love around you.

I see you now at the end of my bed, older by 40 years, grief ugly and pale as death.

I remember you. I remember an angry boy, locked out at 17, stamping and howling 'Let me in' and then your damp beer breath on my face, hard and accusing, your shoulder knocking me down as you bluster up to bed and the worried eye you cast behind you. I heard 'Sorry Mum' but you never said it.

I cried for you and your broken heart. 'Can I come home?' you said with your hurt and your hate and your jealousy scrapping like cats in a sack. We drank a lot that winter and talked until it became light and safe to sleep. You wept on childhood sheets and mowed the lawn. You bought cookery books and spanners and tacked Christmas lights around the porch. You hoovered and decorated until I wanted you to leave.

I wanted you to not be here for this end, to be too busy and inconvenienced, relieved almost, too loved elsewhere.

I gesture for the final dose, it tastes of glass, of light, of silver, sweet as my baby's sleeping forehead, salty as his fingertips. My morphine smile is for your comfort, little boy. I squeeze your hand. Look, I breathe easy. I catch the wind, fill my sails and navigate home.

THE MOTHER THIEF

℧

ALISON WASSELL

Rhona calls me Debbie, which is not my name. I hate her instantly.

'Deborah.' I mutter, sounding even to myself like a surly teenager. She stares at me, smiling slightly, refusing to acknowledge the difference.

She gestures at a chair, simultaneously closing her desk drawer, which contains the remains of her lunchtime salad. Carefully, she dabs at the corners of her mouth with a tissue. I half expect her to take out a mirror and reapply her lipstick before confirming that my mother is dying. She hands over an informative leaflet in which she has helpfully circled in blue biro the stage to which the disease has already silently progressed. She asks if I have any questions. I imagine asking if she knows her blouse makes her look like Margaret Thatcher. She is at least ten years younger than I am. I shake my head.

In the awkward silence, Rhona's eyes travel from my grubby trainers to the unwashed hair I have hurriedly scraped into a ponytail. Summoned at short notice, I have come from teaching a Year Six PE lesson. My mother has told her I work in a school, she says. Her face suggests she is picturing me mopping floors, scrubbing toilets.

'Deputy Head.' I say, and she fails to prevent her eyebrows from rising in disbelief. I take comfort from the fact that there is a clump of couscous on the front of her blouse.

That evening, on the ward, my mother complains that the spaceships landing in the courtyard outside have been keeping her awake. This is new, and terrifies me more than her distended stomach and the feet that are too swollen for slippers. We have inhabited this unfamiliar world of illness for little more than a week, and until today she has greeted each wave of bad news with stoical clichés gleaned over the years from bad novels and soap operas. She has declared herself determined to fight this new affliction. It has been sent to try her. Worse things happen at sea. Well, maybe not to us, but her store of phrases is somewhat depleted. Only yesterday, I cringed and blushed as she told a disinterested nurse that I was her rock. Now she gazes at me with bemused eyes as I mention her treatment. The spacemen are not as green as you might expect, she says, and their leader looks a little like Simon Cowell. Cold fear grips my insides, and a single tear escapes. Momentarily, she is my mother again. She takes my hands in both of hers.

'No, no, no, don't cry,' she pleads. Then something disturbs her thoughts. She leans towards the window, her hand behind her ear in a parody of listening. Can I hear them? They have arrived early tonight.

Even in this strange new world, the days pass as they have always done. Working from old lesson plans, I somehow manage to continue teaching 30 10- and 11-year-olds. I mark their work. I listen to their problems and envy them their trivial preoccupations. In the evenings, I visit my mother. Each time, she relates the details of some new fantasy. She and her fellow patients have been held hostage by an angry clown. Her mother (dead now for ten years) has been to visit her, bringing Marks and Spencer's fruit salad. Sometimes she asks me why I have not been to see her. She has been worried that some disaster has befallen me. After a while, I stop correcting her.

On the first morning of half-term, Rhona telephones me at home. She says that my mother is concerned that I have stopped visiting. I mention her obvious confusion, which Rhona fails to acknowledge. She recognises that I have a busy life, she says. She will not judge me for that. A combination of outrage and hysteria makes me shrill. There is no need to raise my voice, Rhona tells me, having clearly been trained for this kind of encounter. She calls me Debbie again.

For the first time, free from work, I visit in the afternoon. Rhona is at my mother's bedside. Seeing me, she makes no attempt to move. I stand awkwardly behind her, feeling like an intruder. My mother is dozing, and Rhona is holding her hand; stroking it gently with her thumb. A nurse, passing behind her with the drugs trolley, looks at us, then raises her eyes to the ceiling. I wonder what their name for her is, this 'specialist' nurse who has risen so high above their ranks that she is no longer required to wear a uniform.

I edge closer, pulling up a chair at the other side of the bed. Rhona pretends to notice me for the first time. She tells my mother that Debbie has come to see her. It is very kind of Debbie to spare some of her precious time, she says. My mother turns her head towards me. She stares for a moment, puzzled, then turns back towards Rhona, who has not released her grip nor stopped her stroking. They have been having a wonderful chat, Rhona tells me. A nurse summons her to the telephone. I try to take my mother's hand, but she doesn't respond. Her eyes follow Rhona as she strides down the ward, full of her own importance. Is she coming back? Her face is anxious.

The scene is repeated the following day. This time, when I arrive, the curtains are pulled round the bed and I approach stealthily, eavesdropping on the conversation before making myself known. Rhona is telling my mother how beautiful she is. I imagine her stroking her hair.

'I would have loved to have seen you dancing,' she says. My brain replays the details of my mother's life. My father used to joke that she danced like a disabled elephant. I pull the curtain aside, but Rhona does not look up. She is hand holding again. Without speaking, I open the bedside locker and put away the clean nightdresses I have brought. Rhona tells my mother that Debbie is a good girl. My mother says nothing. Her face remains turned toward Rhona. I busy myself with refilling her water jug. Eventually, Rhona looks at her watch. She has somewhere she needs to be. She is important. People need her. She squeezes my mother's hand. She will be back tomorrow.

My mother's eyes are closed. I lean over her.

'It's Deborah.' I whisper. She stirs and opens her eyes. Her brow furrows.

'I knew a Deborah once,' she says.

The next day, before visiting, I tap on the open door of Rhona's office. Mid-phone call, she holds up her hand, indicating that I should wait until she has finished. She is apparently arranging for someone to collect her dry cleaning. Having accomplished this to her satisfaction, she allows me to enter. I broach the subject of my mother's confusion once more. Again, Rhona disregards my question. She and my mother have had some wonderful conversations, she informs me. She smiles. There is an odd look in her eyes, as though she is imagining herself somewhere else. For the first time, I wonder if she is entirely sane.

I try again. Perhaps it is the drugs, I say. Rhona shrugs herself into her jacket, claiming an urgent meeting. My mother is a real lady, she informs me. She ushers me out of the door in front of her. As she edges past me she meets my eye. It is an honour for her to be the one my mother can confide in. Her chin wobbles in a pantomime of holding back tears. She clicks away on her inappropriately high heels.

My mother develops a chest infection. I sit beside her as, semi-conscious, she rasps painfully. Once, waking suddenly and briefly, she asks why it hurts so much. I have no answer. I lay my head next to hers on the pillow and plead with her to let go. Stubborn as ever, she rasps on. I sit for an hour in the hospital canteen, my hands nursing an unwanted mug of coffee. When I return to the ward, she is sitting up, her cheeks pink with fever, her eyes shining. But she is alert. Rhona has taken my chair, and they are giggling together like excited teenagers over some secret joke.

The telephone rings in the early hours of the morning, and I know before answering that the time I have dreaded and wished for has arrived. I speed through deserted streets, ignoring traffic lights, made reckless by impending grief. Arriving at the ward door, I buzz for admittance. Watching through the glass panel as a nurse pads towards me, I realise I am too late. The curtains are drawn around my mother's bed. As I push them aside, Rhona's head jerks towards me, as though my arrival is both unexpected and unwelcome. Nothing about her appearance suggests that these are not her regular working hours. Standing reluctantly, she touches my mother's lifeless hand before moving aside.

'She died in my arms,' she whispers. I imagine tightening the scarf around her neck until her face turns beetroot and she gasps for breath.

Three months later, queuing in a garden centre café, I see her again. She is with an overweight woman in a lilac velour tracksuit, who is paying for her lunch. Our eyes meet, but there is no flicker of recognition. I buy my sandwich and seat myself at an adjacent table. The overweight woman is talking in a too loud voice. Rhona frowns in reprimand.

The woman blushes, apologises, and rummages in her handbag for an envelope, which she hands across the table. Rhona opens it, and glances cursorily at the cute kitten on the card inside. Several ten pound notes flutter onto the table. She leans over and, without warmth, pecks the woman on the cheek. Her mobile buzzes and she reaches eagerly for it.

As she speaks urgently into the phone she rises to her feet, stuffing the notes into her handbag. She leaves the cute kitten in a puddle of spilled tea. Shrugging in mock helplessness she briefly touches the woman's shoulder as she leaves. I wonder if this is some prearranged emergency, designed to save Rhona from her obligatory birthday lunch with the mother who so clearly does not fit her hard-won image. The woman pushes her plate away, her appetite gone. She locates a scrunched up tissue in her bag and blows her nose noisily. I sit down opposite her. She looks a little upset, I tell her, my voice full of concern. I wonder if there is anything I can do to help?

THE GRIEF SCHISM

✧

DAVID MOHAN

This is how it will be, *I think*, my mind
a bible for how to breathe when the sun goes in,
when the rain begins to claim its kingdom.

I cannot live in this, *I say*, speaking
to the silent kitchen, letting each word
blow out like smoke-rings practised for no one.

There must be a way round this, *I write*,
expanding a list that starts and ends
with death. I have books of letters,

diaries, I have parts of your love
spread out so thin I cannot remember
whose life I live in. I sip tea

in the manner of the past, the thought
comes to me that this is *living on* –
I live on, *on* being how the past extends

its legacy in time. But I am
no longer warm in the skin you knit,
no longer satisfied, how would you

say it, what words would you choose,
to speak this moment,
what words are left to me to say it for us both.

How and long, I will come through
questions and live in the pause,
all dark deferred.

I make many starts at grief,
all false, all loose as thought.
I need to found my own religion

to bear this out.

SPOONS

ℰℐ

PETE BUCKINGHAM

They had always had a big king size bed, a car park a friend had called it. He looked at it now with her in it, curled up in her favourite position. He stopped and watched her, her still body unmoving under the sheet. He thought back to the first time her had seen her in that position, in a much smaller bed, the memory made him warm an echo of a long lost power, now only the memory generated the heat his body remained cool.

Still watching her, he reached over for his mug, hot, steaming, strong tea, a little milk and no sugar. He had always drank it like that, the heat from the mug stung his hand but he held onto it knowing it would pass glad of a sensation of some sort. He recalled a passage in a film where the hero's mate was dying and the hero wanted to help his mate's pain, his mate had replied that pain was good as it meant he was alive; he had laughed at that but now he understood. He thanked God that his mind still worked and he still had his memories even if his body was failing him.

He raised the mug to his lips, drank the tea it was hot in his mouth, it was hot as it drained down his throat and into his stomach he winced with a mixture of pain and pleasure, memories cascaded one upon the other following the tea down into his body. The first time she had given him a cup of tea in the canteen where she had worked, her finger had touched his deliberately she had given him a smile and touched his finger tip with hers his whole body had been swallowed up with a wave of nuclear heat radiating inwards from his finger he had rushed to sit down before his manhood had betrayed his desire.

He drank more tea, cooler now, he remembered their first time, hot excited white heat-crazed passion unable to think of anything else he had been pure untouched she was not, she had liked that encouraging him teaching him slowly allowing her advantage to be given away to be replaced with a mutual desire so strong it hurt. To be away to be separated to be with parents, friends others not him or her had been pain only wanting to be together to be one so so so many times.

He shuddered the pain inside, dying from within, it hurt but he had got used to it, accepted it, the counsellor had told him to accept. Bollocks to that fight fight fight all of his life before he met her, she had changed him calmed him gave him something he did not know he didn't have or even wanted. The counsellor had been right accepting his future had made him free, given him strength to continue to live his life how he wanted to. Only she had been able to do that for him before, with her everything had made sense.

More tea cooler still now and with cooler memories, wedding night, first home, first baby then the second, how could he have been so blessed to have helped create those two, see them grow up become adults, have families of their own leave him and her alone growing older but closer still, holidays fun times parties dancing walking loving, another shudder inside this time the pain was from the memories, pain is good it means you are alive, his mind still good having decided and taking the actions himself.

Tea is cold but he drinks it, her illness started slowly, first a silly mistake, a couple of accidents, check up look up join up, fight the thing by attending committees, raising awareness, shouting about it all the while slowly fading away from him a piece at a time. She needs more meds, can't drive now, can't sleep can't wake pretending for the kids and for him but he sees, knows feels pretends she is OK the big story was he protecting their love or was their love protecting them. The slow disintegration in her slowly taking her then suddenly it was him urgent appointments why had he not seen his GP he could have had more years, he had thought of that more years long years grandchildren years but years without her he had decided quickly, no more fight left acceptance of his decision his children will understand, the letter was short no apologies play the file in the PC.

His tea was drunk he put down his mug, onto the coaster as always, he curled up onto their bed fitting alongside her as tight as two spoons in a drawer, he could smell her scent he could feel her skin his knees came up into her knees he stroked her hair, they were teenagers again loving one another his memories were good only his body was failing the tablet working now, now he would join her.

Spoons.

THE WAITING ROOM

ᔆᔆ

HARRIET DAVIES

My mum and I sat in the depressing canteen, a few patients around us with family members – who was which I didn't know – ordering our sad little jacket potatoes and quiches. It was like being back at a school canteen, except with death hanging over you. I envied the doctors and nurses their neutral attitudes, their objective positions. It was work for them. My mum sat opposite me eating, smiling when she looked up into my eyes. I held her hand across the table and looked back into her eyes. She pointed between us, as if motioning that we were together, and just said 'nice'. Some tears came to her eyes and I gulped back mine. 'Yes, it's lovely mum,' I replied.

We had been there five hours already, and there was no TV, and she couldn't read or talk, so I had sat next to her all morning, flicking through magazines, hoping she would doze off so I could read to pass the endless day in the sickening glare of the hospital lighting.

After lunch I took her out for a small walk. I was getting a headache. We walked round and round the tiny square in front of the hospital. It was in central London but this little square with the hospital in it was hushed, protected from the business of London because there was no point in looking nice, being successful or being rich when you were dying. It was like an unpleasant haven from the mania of the city. We walked around, my mum with her coat over her face like an Eskimo, me trying to guide her, arm in arm, and hating life. The trees were bare and black, their branches like knuckles, the air was freezing, and I really did hate it all. It was all so cold and hard as we shuffled around.

'Daddy,' my mum said out of nowhere. What was she thinking? I wondered. I held her tighter.

After the walk we went back to the canteen for tea and she kept holding my hand, smiling and saying 'nice'. Afterwards was back to the waiting room again where we sat waiting forever for her brain scan. Patients were given these big arm chairs, as if they were in a living room reserved for them, and little meals on trays were brought in for them at lunch time. I sat next to my mum in a plastic chair all day. She suddenly sat up at one point and seemed to see something that surprised her, and she traced it with her hand as if following a falling light. She seemed entranced and said 'pretty' as she looked at nothing, then she looked at me and I think she realised she had imagined it and seemed embarrassed. I didn't care if she imagined it, as long as it was nice. She could be in whatever reality except this one as far as I was concerned. I just didn't want her to know the abject hopelessness and humiliation of her disease.

Later on, as we tried to get the train home my oyster card beeped and had run out of money. My mum was trapped on the other side of the barrier and the commuter crowds were washing her away towards the elevator. I was screaming at people, 'she's ill, she's ill!' but no one paid any attention, as they cursed me for blocking the barrier in their rush home. Thankfully a transport worker saw me and grabbed my mum and I explained to her the situation. She was so lovely, as she stood holding my mum and pointing at me as I topped up my oyster so that she wouldn't be afraid, that I got a huge lump in my throat.

That day, I hated God. I didn't really believe in him but I had to have somewhere to direct my hate. I hated everyone else too. I was exhausted from sitting all day, and racked by guilt – because it's never, ever enough. No matter what I did I couldn't alleviate the awfulness of what was happening.

The day I had found out my mum had Alzheimer's disease, the previous July I think – although weirdly I can't be sure – I was hungover. It was a shock because she was only 54, but her behaviour had been changing for years. She had been forgetting things and saying the same few things over and over again, until her speech had been reduced to a few words only. Maybe I knew but I certainly didn't want to believe it; I didn't want to believe it was anything irreversible. Because that would mean, really, that she was already lost.

The night before I found out, the night when her test results were being delivered, I got drunk. I didn't call home; I forgot about it. My family insists I didn't forget, that I couldn't cope so I escaped from it, but I think I forgot. In the morning I couldn't remember anything from the night before, except one of my bosses at work putting me into a cab and ordering the driver to take me home. God, how awful. I woke up trying not to piece the night together, but the humiliation of my drunken behaviour burned in my brain. My sister walked into my room. 'How come you're here?' I asked. 'It's mum,' she said, 'we got the results back from her test yesterday and it is Alzheimer's.' 'Oh my God, I was so drunk last night,' I groaned, rolling over into my covers. 'So what? It doesn't matter, don't you understand what I'm telling you?' my sister shouted at me. 'I can't deal with this,' I said, picking up my phone to call my boss. 'Will, my mum has Alzheimer's. I feel fucked up. I don't know when I'll be in work,' I said, trying hard not to cry. Then I cried a bit; nothing felt real.

The day was hot. My sister and her boyfriend had come round to mine the night before and stayed with my house mate, waiting for me to come home to break the news. But of course I hadn't come home, not till long after they were asleep. They had called people in the family, aunts, uncles and my dad, who was divorced many years ago from my mum, and talked about things. I had done nothing.

'Dad's coming to meet us for coffee,' my sister told me.

Later, we sat outside the Royal Festival Hall. We were at the back, where it faces South, and the sun glared down on my unwashed, hungover body, big sunglasses covering my face and the fact I was a fucking mess. My dad arrived and we sat there, unsure what to talk about under the circumstances. In shock, of course. We ordered breakfast. I remember my sister and my dad having a stupid argument, over when she would have her coffee. She wanted it then and he told the waiter to bring it after the meal, then my sister insisted to the poor waiter to bring it now, and my dad said to her in his stern, headmaster's voice, 'We'll discuss this later.' At which point she burst into tears and shouted that we wouldn't discuss it fucking later because she didn't give a shit and there were bigger problems. 'Be nice to her!' I interjected, shouting at my dad. He seemed to realise he was wrong but was too proud to say sorry so we all just dropped it. I was in hell, or the closest I've come to it in my life. Other people lived; I just seemed to travel through time. After breakfast I walked across Waterloo Bridge with my dad. The city looked painfully idyllic on such a summery day.

After that day I spent weeks on the sofa. I had spent my life being determined not to be my mum. She had spent her life in bouts of depression, sitting on our sofa crying. Letting our house fall apart while lamenting the bloody past. 'If only my parents hadn't died when I was young,' she would say, 'If only I hadn't married your father.' If bloody only. I hated her for it. But, I saw now, I could never have even begun to understand.

Eventually I went back to work but would sit at my desk for hours doing nothing, and I was hours late most mornings. At night I couldn't sleep and I would toss and turn in bed, searching desperately for a thought that was comforting, that I could bear thinking, and trying to push away all the thoughts that haunted me: images of my mum's brain on a scan, bits turning black, dying. Those pockets were *her*, I thought. They were who she was. Thoughts of her losing more and more control over her body plagued me, or how my children would never know her, as I had never known her parents. And the worst was what a tragedy her life had been, or maybe it was how scared and lost she might feel.

I was tormented by these thoughts every night and I would stay awake until the early hours, when the world is utterly still and mocks your fears with its silence. Two a.m. is a dark time. My body ached all over. I was so tired I couldn't work out if it was my body or mind which was tired or awake, but something kept me up. I feared sleep because all my dreams were nightmares. They were of extremes: at night I found myself leaning over great heights, or in burning heat, objects were being hurled at me, or I was swimming in the streets of London flooded with dirty water. In all of them the landscapes were utterly deserted except for me. Otherwise I dreamt horrible things about my body, my teeth crumbling into my hands, bleeding from the mouth. Then in the morning I couldn't wake up. There were many days when I woke up knowing I couldn't face it, when I was awoken by the tears running down my face, streaming into the pillow.

It turned to winter, one of the coldest in many, many years, and the skies were always white. My bed was by the window at that time, in a little North London flat, and I would often put out my arm, glimpse under the blind and see the pale sky and retreat under my cover. A blackness had dawned over my life. My head was fuzzy in the day, overly active all night. Sometimes I wanted to live and wanted life to be better, other times, I lay with my eyes closed and thought of the bliss of non-existence.

One Monday morning I woke up and, as if torn from a womb, I crawled, bleary-eyed into the shower. Hot water, then tea. Liquids coursed over and through my body, and I began slowly to humanise. Cell by cell my consciousness returned and I became dimly aware of reality: the day staring me in the face. 'Get through the day, get through the day.' I clung to this mantra like a frail, ancient lady to a walking stick. I got the train to work, on time for the first time in ages, and stared out of the window – at the suburban shrubbery that grows along a railway line, and at the dead space of London, the greyness of grit piles and box buildings. But this scene, deeply ugly and mundane, comforted me. Once the day was over I went home, exhausted. But another day was over and I had done all I needed to, and there are times when that is enough.

Since then, nearly two years have passed. She is still ill and I am momentarily struck by depression and guilt, and a lot of the time I block it out. Sometimes I wish she would die sooner so I could grieve properly, so I could remember her properly, so I could be free from it. I am a terrible daughter. But if I skip to the end it's because I'm afraid of what's in between. The thing is, religion and societies have an answer to death, but what about when someone is still here but lost? I often think 'this isn't my mum', but then, who is she? Meanwhile, she looks at me and calls me her mum, whom she lost when she was my age. So I, like my children if I have them, never knew my grandma. And my fragmented memories of her memories are all I have to piece together something about where I came from, and they are as ethereal and fragile as the glittering lights she saw that day in the hospital waiting room.

PAPIER MACHÉ DOLL

❧

AMANDA BOWDEN

I pull my long black woollen coat around me. Lennon lies quietly at my feet, the cold air teasing his fur. My sister tells me it's disrespectful to take a dog to a funeral. I don't see why. It's a woodland funeral. Dad's in a wicker coffin. She doesn't like that either, Jasmine. God only knows how she turned out so conventionally; so staid, so normal.

Twanged notes play with the still air – Evan on the five-stringed banjo. Dad's banjo. He finishes the song, pauses then throws the banjo into the grave. It thuds and gives off a final note. Jasmine pulls a face like she's tasted something nasty.

The grave is starting to look like a white elephant stall. So far it contains – as well as dad – a flat cap, a scarf, a necklace, a coin, a crystal, a belt buckle, several CDs and photos, football programmes, a CND badge and the banjo.

I finger my offering in my deep pocket. My sister steps forward and throws in a long-stemmed white lily. Very traditional. Very her. From my pocket I pull my doll that looks like it's been made and painted by a child. I'd stayed up until 3 a.m. trying to perfect one. Then I'd stopped. Dad wasn't flawless, neither am I. Nor is dear Jasmine, much as she likes to think she is. So I picked the first one I'd made; the most imperfect. Dad would like that one best.

We used to make them as kids. It's my first recollection of childhood; sitting in the tiny kitchen in our council flat on stools making those dolls. We would take them, with whatever else we could muster, to Greenham Common. I didn't really understand the relevance of the place then. To me it was just like a big picnic on a huge campsite. We'd rock up in our VW van held together with rust and proudly displaying large CND symbols either side – which always reminded me of a bird's foot.

1981. I was eight years old when the protest march was organised. I didn't witness it but I imagine it was a phenomenal sight. I can't think of something like that happening nowadays; the march maybe, but not the peace camp. I loved it there. It got bigger each time we visited. It was such a unique atmosphere; more than community spirit. People gathered for a common cause. It was family. Jasmine hated it. She would've been 12 going on 20; too old to play and too young to be taken seriously. Not that she was interested in campaigning. Heaven forbid she should get her manicured hands dirty. I often thought she was adopted. She should've been. She split our family more than unified it.

Mine is the last memento in the grave. For the wake I'd arranged a picnic in the woods. Jasmine decides not to stay, mumbles something about work commitments. Doesn't want to risk getting a speck of dirt on her Karen Millen or Jane Norman, more like. When she first spoke so fondly of Karen and Jane, I actually thought they were friends. I don't do designer. All my clothes are from charity shops. The coat she wore today probably totals the cost of my entire wardrobe. I'm not jealous. I just don't get it. If I had that kind of money I'd buy a piece of art from a local artist. Like me.

We move away from the grave, Lennon at my heels, and settle in a beautiful spot. The bright green grass is short and spotted with daisies. Tall trees surround the glade, their bronzing leaves rustle in the autumnal breeze. The odd acorn and conker lay on the floor. A low seasonal sun bleeds through branches, comfortingly warm.

People unroll blankets and unwrap food. Bags and boxes of rolls, scones, cakes, samosas, cold pizza and stuff I don't recognise are passed around. Beer is opened, wine uncorked, thermos flasks circulated. Stories are swapped and memories shared accompanied by laughter. It's not a jovial atmosphere, but it's not sad either. As the sun sinks, the chill air increases and people begin packing up and hugging goodbye. Lennon is sated and sleepy from copious titbits. His Dennis Healey Westie eyebrows lift as movement disturbs him. I'm asked countless times if I will be okay, do I want a bed for the night, company, a lift home? I thank them all and politely decline.

Lennon and I trail back to the car park with the last of the mourners and friends. I unlock my bike, take my gloves, lights and helmet from the pannier then scoop up Lennon. Wrapping his fleecy blanket around him, I clip him into the dog carrier on the handlebars.

It doesn't bother me going back to the empty house. I'd moved back in with dad when mum died of breast cancer. I'd had over a week to get used to it being without him now. I had contemplated moving the furniture or getting rid of dad's chair; the tatty armchair that he always sat in by the fire with Lennon at his feet on the rug. The chair I had found him in ten days ago. Dead. A peaceful death, they said. Massive brain haemorrhage in his sleep. He was always nodding off reading *Private Eye*. I got used to leaving him there. He'd wake when the fire died down and he got cold, and take himself off to bed.

Apparently they are more common than you think – aneurysms. Loads of people wake up next to dead people. That must be awful. That morning was bad enough. I remember seeing him as I got to the bottom of the stairs and chastising him for being there all night. I remember having a cold feeling in my stomach, thinking the dog was dead because initially he didn't respond to my voice, didn't lift his head. 'Come on, sleepy head.' I nudged dad. I remember simultaneously feeling relief and horror – is that possible? – as Lennon lifted his head and dad slumped forward, his lips blue. He was so cold. I sat on the floor with Lennon and held dad's stiffening fingers. Eventually, through streaming tears I got up and unfolded a blanket from the back of the chair and tucked it round him. Stupid really.

I phoned my sister. She was a big help. Cold, I mean calm – Freudian slip. I said, 'Jas, dad's dead.' She said, 'Call an ambulance, they'll deal with it.' I said, '*It?*' she sighed and said, 'Take him away.' I said, 'I don't want him taken away.' She said, 'Oh for God's sake, P. Grow up.' Then she went quiet for a bit and I tried not to sob audibly. Eventually, she told me she would ring later, when I had calmed down, and check how I was doing. Perhaps she did her crying when she hung up. I stood staring at the phone for a bit. Then Lennon nudged my leg. I had to think hard to remember the number for the ambulance; funny that 999 can be difficult to recall. She was nice, the lady on the other end. She'd woken up next to her dead husband. See what I mean?

Jasmine rang later to check on me. I was sat in the dark on the rug by the fire with Lennon. Couldn't bring myself to sit in dad's chair. She didn't ask how I was or if *it* had been *dealt* with. She said something about assuming I would know of his funeral arrangements as he'd not discussed them with her, and to tell her when and where, she'd be there.

I still can't sit in that chair. It smells of him. Which is odd because I can't say I noticed him smelling of anything specific when he was alive, expect maybe Imperial Leather soap. The chair doesn't smell of that though. It smells of comfort, love and tenderness and deep rooted principles and bucking the system. And contentment. It smells mostly of that; a life well lived.

I'm sat on the grey-white sheepskin rug with Lennon when she arrives. I've just finished making paper knots and laying the kindle. It's oddly therapeutic, almost creative. Haven't been creative since I found him. Didn't open my stall this week. All I've done are those bloody papier maché dolls and I cocked that up.

She gives her usual cursory distasteful glance of the place when I let her in.

'Do you want a drink? I've no milk. There's rum, and wine.'

'I'm not stopping. Can you put a decent light on?'

'Sit down,' I offer, switching on the standard lamp.

She purses her lips into a pencil-thin line as she takes in the debris of pottery and papier maché on the kitchen table. It's never been used for eating; we always ate off our laps. She almost sits in dad's chair, but doesn't. Clipping open her, doubtless, designer bag, she pulls out an envelope.

'I'm to show you this,' she clears her throat as she speaks and proffers the envelope, watches me tear it open.

As I pull out the contents, I see the words Adoption and Birth Certificate.

'So, you *are* adopted?' I speak before looking properly.

'No,' she snorts. 'You are.'

I yank out the rest of the paperwork and skim it.

She's by the front door when she turns and concedes, 'I can see why you'd think that.'

Then I notice it, dad's name on my birth certificate.

'But...' I can't find the words.

'Dad had a fling. *Your* mum died after having you, some sort of complication,' she waves her hand dismissively. '*My* mum adopted you. Christ knows why.'

'You really hate me, don't you?' I whisper.

She pauses, front door ajar, 'No, Peony. I resent you. I hate him, and as for her...'

'Hate is so harsh. You don't come to the funeral of someone you hate.'

Jasmine turns to face me, her expression hidden in the shadow of the doorway.

'I'm angry. I've been angry since the day you arrived. They doted on you. They were so protective of you.'

'They would've doted on you, given half a chance. You were always so...unapproachable.'

'I was pushed out. Maybe I'm jealous, if I'm honest. There – happy? Look, I've kept my promise and the stupid secret. I've done what I said I would. That's an end to it.'

'You've known all this time and didn't say anything? I can't imagine how hard that must have been for you, and painful.'

'Shut up, P. Don't pretend you know me,' her voice falters. Then with renewed vigour, Jasmine flings the door open and cold air rushes in.

'Jasmine, wait. Maybe we can...'

She cuts me dead with a hollow laugh, 'Oh, please don't say start again.'

'But we're family. That's got to matter.'

'My family are dead. Keep the house, I want no part of it and have no reason to visit it.' She slams the door behind her. I listen to her heels clip up the garden path then she's gone. Silence engulfs me.

In a trance, I lay and light the fire; watch the flames dance and tease their way up the chimney. The fire cracks, jolting me back to reality. I get up to make a coffee. On the kitchen table lay four papier maché dolls. Scooping them up, I carry them to the fire. I lean over Lennon, catatonic on the rug, and line them up on the mantelpiece. Mum, Dad, Peony, Jasmine. Must make one for Lennon.

Tearing the adoption papers up, I throw them on the fire. We are family, whatever Jas says. So she's angry. So she resents me. But she never said a word in all that time. We had some humdinger fights as kids. She'd had this ammo against me all that time and not used it. Surely that must count for something. One day I'll find out.

BASEBALL CARDS

ᘡᔕ

LEISSA SHAHRAK

I can't think good. The doc knows I can't think good but I don't need him to tell me. I just can't think like I used to. My wife doesn't cook now. She takes me to the dining room here to eat all the time. The dining room has pictures of flowers on the wall. They bring me a bib and juice. One guy here eats the same thing every day—fish. He is bald and he says hi to us. My wife says hi to him. I say do you have fish again? I want to eat but not fish. I don't like fish now. I did or maybe I didn't like it in the past. I say I want meat. M—E—A—T. Meat. No fish. My wife tells the girl to bring me meat and juice and something else. What was it?

The guy with the fish says he does not like juice. I can't spell juice. I can't think good now. I wish I could play cards. My wife says I have to eat. I say I want to play cards to make her think I can. I know I can't play cards anymore. My wife says I have to eat. She puts the bib on me. I say I do not want this bib. But my wife never listens. She sits down and says you have to have a bib Bob. You don't want to get your shirt dirty. I say how do you know what I want? My wife thinks she knows everything because we've been married forever. I know what I want. I want to play cards.

A girl with purple fingernails comes and hands me pills. I throw them in my mouth and she says you missed one. She kneels on the floor to look for it. She says Bob you are a case you know. What did you do with that pill? The girls here pick on me. I like to pick on them. I say I don't want this fish.

She says it is not fish. I say it is but I know it's not. She says is not. I say is too. She says is not and hands me a blue pill. I say I won't take this pill it was on the floor. She says it was not. I say you like to pick on me don't you? She says it's not the pill on the floor. I wouldn't give you a dirty one. I take the blue pill and this time I throw it up and catch it in my mouth. I say it's a goner.

A woman with big lips parks her walker at the next table and starts to sing. She sings swing low sweet chariot comin' for to carry me home. I tell my wife that woman is a good-looking woman. My wife doesn't say anything. I say I like that song and I wave to the woman. She stops singing and waves back. My wife says eat your food Bob. I whistle at the woman but she doesn't do anything. I tell my wife it's her fault because she didn't comb my hair. My wife makes me mad. The guy with the fish says here have some fish. I don't like fish. I tell the guy I don't like fish. My wife says eat your meat Bob. I eat.

I have ice cream and my wife says we can go now. I say where? She says back to our place. I say I want to get out of this place. She says we live here now and wheels me back. In our place there are old pictures of babies. I don't know their names but my wife does. I'm tired and I want to go to bed. My wife says I should sit in my chair and watch the baseball game. I say my back hurts. She says the pill will work soon. My back hurts but I sit in my chair so my wife won't scold me. Sometimes my wife is mean. I say I am tired of baseball and I want to play cards. She says she doesn't have any cards.

I am mad at my wife. I turn my chair around and wheel over to look out at the birds. They eat seed my wife puts outside. More birds come now. The trees are green and the birds eat seed. S—E—E—D. Seed. One bird has red wings. It's small and sings. I like the bird. I say hey come watch the birds with me. My wife likes the birds too. I tell her the birds need more food. My wife says she fed them this morning. I don't believe her. I say the birds are hungry and they don't have food. My wife says if it makes you happy I'll give them more food. She puts more seed out. It doesn't make me happy. I want to play cards. I tell my wife. She doesn't say anything. I know I can't play cards now. I used to know where all the cards were. I used to know who had them and if they had played them. Now I don't. I don't know my own cards. I miss cards.

My wife opens the door and says look one of our girls is here. It's the one with frizzy hair. I know my girls—two of them. But I think we had three or four. Five maybe. And maybe one boy. I say to my girl when did you get here? She says just now and how are you? I say still here and then I say you need to comb your hair. She says there's a lot of wind out there. I say why are you here? She says to see you. What did you eat? I say I don't know. Fish. She says I thought you don't like fish. I say I do like fish. But I don't. I say your mother won't let me play cards and I think we should get a divorce. My girl says after 60 years? I say we've been married forever. I tell her my wife hides the cards. She says oh, Dad, surely not. I say you need to get me out of here and get my watch fixed. She looks at my watch. She says it's working fine, Dad. I don't believe her. I say look at the birds. She looks. Two birds are fighting over the seed. I say see they are hungry and they need more food. My wife says I just fed them. She says they have plenty of food. The birds leave. I look at my girl and I say I need to take a nap now. She says you don't need to stay up for me. She looks at my wife and says oh let him go to bed.

They help me get in bed. I know it is my bed. It has a blue blanket with clouds on it. I tell my wife to get in too but she wants to stay up to talk. I say you talk all the time. She does. She talks on the phone and to all the people here all the time. My wife just laughs. I say I think we should get a divorce. My girl looks at my wife and rolls her eyes. I tell my wife that she lost my cards and we don't have a thing in common. My wife laughs again and puts my blanket on me. She never listens.

I tell my wife to move the bed down. I say I don't like this rabbit hole I'm in. She moves the bed down but I'm still in the rabbit hole. I tell her to move it all the way down. She says you need your legs up a little. I say I do not and I tell her again. I. Do. Not. Like. This. Rabbit. Hole. She moves the bed a little but I'm still in the rabbit hole. I shout damn it I want out of this rabbit hole. She moves the bed again but she doesn't do it right. I say I'm fed up with lying in this rabbit hole and why did you hide my cards. I want a divorce. She says I'll lower your legs just a little and put your head all the way down how's that? I say terrible. I say I'm going to get out of this bed right now. I swing my legs over the side of the bed. My wife shouts Bob you'll fall. My girl says don't, Dad, we'll fix it. She makes me lie down. I tell my wife if you don't get me out of this rabbit hole, I'm going to holler as loud as I can. My wife knows I'll do that. She knows I can still holler. My girl says hush, Dad, do you want me to try, Mom? My wife doesn't listen to her. She moves the bed and she says Bob now your bed is just like the doctor at the VA wants it and you know you have to obey the VA's orders. I feel tired. I know I should follow the VA's orders so I lay flat and say OK. My wife is mean sometimes but I don't know what I'd do without her. I grab her hand and ask her to turn on the TV please. She does and the two of them start to go out to the other room. I say don't forget to feed the birds. F—E—E—D. Feed. My wife says I won't forget I promise.

I am alone and I look at the baseball game on TV for a minute. I'm too tired to watch. I look at my hands on the blanket and check them. Ten fingers. I raise up the blanket to check under it. Two legs, ten toes, two balls, and one penis. All in order. I close my eyes and try to think of birds but I wish I could play cards and now I can see the cards in my hand—the jack of hearts and the queen of spades but I don't like the queen of spades and I hear my bridge partner say what a catch and he says wow I thought he'd make it all the way around the diamond on that one and I know he's telling me to slough off that little trey of diamonds I have in my hand and then I hear my partner say something about coming out of the club house and I know that clubs are trumps and I should play a club but I can't see my cards so good now and I try to think what to play next when my partner says it's in left field it's a goner and I know for sure I don't have any more tricks left and I know in the end we will lose no matter what I play and I tell my partner that I'm sorry I didn't play it better and we lost. I just don't think so good now.

ABOUT THE AUTHORS

❧

Janette Ayachi is an Edinburgh-based poet with a combined honours degree from Stirling University and a Masters in Creative Writing from Edinburgh University. She has been widely published in over 40 literary journals and anthologies, shortlisted for a few awards including: Write Queer London, a Lancelot Andrewes Award and currently StAnza Digital Slam 2013. She is the author of two poetry collections: *Pauses at Zebra Crossings* and *A Choir of Ghosts*, and editor of *The Undertow Review*, an online Arts and Lits Journal.

❧

Sarah Bakewell was born in Manchester and is currently a student of English and Creative Writing at the University of Salford. Writing has been her passion since childhood and she was initially inspired by Jacqueline Wilson and Jill Murphy.

❧

Helen Barnes grew up in Nottingham and has lived in South East London for most of the last 30 years. She is a psychotherapist in training and a social policy researcher. *Leave-taking* is her first published fiction.

❧

Amanda Bowden has been writing for a number of years and has had success in short story competitions and a novel writing competition. Currently running a therapy centre and teaching Pilates, Amanda dreams of becoming a full-time writer one day. In her role as a hypnotherapist, Amanda works mainly with depressed, stressed and anxious clients. She has developed an interest in and writes a lot about coping with death and surviving life!

❧

Pete Buckingham has been happily married for 34 years to his wife Carole. They live in Cheshire and have two grown children and two grandchildren. He likes gardening, dancing and swimming, recently completing the one mile swim at Salford Quays. He is a volunteer counsellor at St Luke's Hospice in Winsford and Survive Sexual Abuse service in Crewe.

⟨⟩

Harriet Davies is a 27-year-old journalist living in London. She studied at Sussex University and has a Masters in Economics, and her ultimate ambition is to write a full-length novel.

⟨⟩

Alva de Chiro was born and educated in Chesterfield, trained as a teacher in London and, with gaps to raise a family, taught for 31 years. She married an Italian man so has a close affinity with Southern Italy. Alva is now a widow. On retiring she began to attend writing, botanical drawing and calligraphy classes, and to do volunteer work with a partially sighted group. She gives talks to a variety of groups and so raises money for the local hospice, where her husband died. She has spoken on Radio Derby about Dignity in Dying.

⟨⟩

Kit de Waal writes flash fiction, short stories and longer form prose. She is published in *The Fish Anthology*, *Tindal Street Fiction Group Anthology* and *Black & Blue Writing*. She writes non-fiction on children and adoption, is a mentor and editor for other writers and a Trustee of Prisoners Abroad. Kit is also a member of Tindal Street Fiction Group, Oxford Narrative Group and WRB Writers. She lives in London and Leamington Spa.

⟨⟩

Maureen Gallagher's short stories, literary criticism and poetry have been published in magazines and journals worldwide. She has been shortlisted or won many awards for her work, most recently the Cúirt International Short Story Award. In 2011 she won both the Goldsmith Poetry and Swift Satire awards. Maureen is an able performer of her work and has been broadcast on RTE. Her first collection of poetry, *Calling the Tune*, was published by Wordsonthestreet Press in December 2008.

⟨⟩

Dr Faye Gishen is a Consultant Physician in Palliative Medicine in North London. Her specialist interests are in cancer survivorship, medical education and pastoral care of doctors and other healthcare professionals. Her story *The Patient That Changed Me* is based on a real patient whom Faye looked after near the beginning of her specialist training in palliative care: a case that had a marked influence on her subsequent development as a doctor

೧

Sali Gray, juggler extraordinaire and eternal optimist, lives her life to the full and loves every single second of it. As a qualified life and business coach and Cambridge diet consultant, she helps others set and achieve their goals. A passionate writer, public speaker and time philanthropist, Sali created and continues to organise the annual Pink Car Rally for the Little Princess Trust charity, which gives 'real hair' wigs to children who have lost their hair, primarily through cancer treatments.

೧

Josephine Howard taught secondary pupils for 20 years until serious ill health forced her to take early retirement. She wrote her first novel during a protracted convalescence. Josephine joined a WEA group and was encouraged to try her hand at poetry. To her amazement she has, over the years, won several prizes. She is still writing novels and continues to use poetry writing as a valuable form of therapy. Royalties from Josephine's work raise money for charity.

೧

John Hunt spent over 30 years in hospice and palliative care as a clinical nurse, manager and director of care services. Throughout, he continued to work directly with patients and families and it is those relationships which have influenced his writing. He now works for a Catholic charity as a general manager in a care home, in the south of England.

೧

Nick Jarvis has, since graduating from Falmouth University in 2010, been performing poetry and running workshops on writing and identity in venues around the UK. He has recently been published in *Far Off Places, Lavender Review, Gitterwolf,* and *The Parabola Project*. He lives in 'The Town of Books' and works in a castle.

೧

Claire Jones is an underachieving genius who lives with her husband and children in Birmingham. She is interested in the little details of life and finds inspiration in the ordinary. Her poetry blog www.thehungrypoet. co.uk is woefully neglected. She holds degrees in Speech Pathology and English Literature. Aside from writing, her hobbies include allotment gardening and red wine. Her ambitions are to teach creative writing and to eventually finish the washing. She collects teacups and tattoos and cooks a mean quiche.

ço

Kylie Joyce's first attempt at creative writing was at the age of seven, when her poem *The Sea* was read out in her infant school assembly. She has been using writing as a creative outlet ever since. After a varied career, in numerous locations, Kylie has returned to her childhood town and is thoroughly enjoying life in the beautiful county of Devon, where she has recently resumed her writing.

ço

Adam Lound is a Respiratory Physiotherapist who helps run rehabilitation programmes for people with chronic lung disease. He has particular interest in breathlessness, patient education and end of life care. When he's not working, Adam writes stories and screenplays that seem to find themselves revolving around the experiences of characters that are old, sick or unlucky in love. He is currently working on his first feature length screenplay.

ço

Anneliese Mackintosh's short stories have appeared in *The Best British Short Stories 2013*, *Edinburgh Review*, *Gutter*, *Causeway/Cabhsair* and elsewhere. Her fiction has been broadcast on BBC Radio 4 and BBC Radio Scotland. In 2012 she was shortlisted for the Bridport Prize and won first prize for the Unbound Press Short Story Award. Her debut short story collection will be published by Freight in 2014. She lives in Manchester and her website is at www.anneliesemackintosh.com.

ço

Carole Mansur lives in London where she now works with primary age children – and loves it.

ço

David Mohan is based in Dublin, Ireland, and received a PhD in English Literature from Trinity College. He has been published in *Stirring*, *Poetry Salzburg Review*, *New World Writing*, *Contrary*, *Word Riot* and *elimae*. In 2012 he won the Café Writers' International Poetry Competition. He has been shortlisted in the Bridport Prize and nominated for the Pushcart Prize.

ço

Sue Moorhouse had three children's fantasy books published for schools in the 1980s and a prize-winning short story published by Victor Gollancz. Currently she has returned to writing after retiring and had a book of modernised, funny fairy tales written from the old characters' viewpoint published by Ecanus and on Amazon.

જ

Alexandra Obee was born in Surrey in 1985. She became fascinated by people and their lives whilst living abroad as a child, she ultimately studied to become a doctor. She remains a keen traveller, with a particular love of Africa where she has swum with great white sharks and bungy jumped off Victoria Falls – the latter of which still gives her nightmares! *The Night Shift That Changed Me* was inspired by the death of her maternal grandfather whilst she was working in a Birmingham hospital.

જ

Christopher Owen's *An Honourable Life* won first prize in the Final Chapters competition. Christopher has had plays professionally produced including *A Wilde Affair*; *Right ho, Wodehouse!*; *The Real King Kong* and *Still Waters*. Also produced have been *A Family Affair* and *Beware! Danger Zone!* In 2013 *A Parson's Tale* toured NW England. In October 2013 *Women's Voices* by Susan K. Monson and Christopher was produced in Manchester by The New Live Theatre Company. Website is at www.christopherowen.co.uk.

જ

Brenda Read-Brown worked for many years as an IT project manager. She gave this up in 2001 to work as a full-time freelance writer: it seemed a sensible career move at the time. Brenda has won a number of poetry slams, and has performed in many venues in the United Kingdom and abroad. She works in schools, hospitals, prisons and GP surgeries, with older people, in libraries and at festivals. Helping other people find their words is what makes her life a continuing joy.

જ

Leissa Shahrak holds degrees in English and French Literature. Of *Baseball Cards* she says 'Writing from the point-of-view of a character with Alzheimer's Disease was painfully easy. My 91-year-old father suffers from dementia. This story was written in his honor.' Ms Shahrak lives in Kansas City, Missouri, USA where she is currently working on a novel in which three characters struggle to survive in Esfahan, Iran, during the last days of the Pahlevi dynasty.

&

Caroline Sposto writes essays, fiction and poetry. Her work has run in *The Saturday Evening Post, Family Circle* magazine and a wide variety of literary magazines and anthologies in the US, Canada and the UK. In 2013, she won the silver medal in the Great American Think-off, an amateur philosophy competition. She lives with her husband in Memphis, Tennessee where she is an active community volunteer. Their two grown daughters live in New York City.

&

Gráinne Tobin lives in Newcastle, Co Down. She is a member of Belfast's Word of Mouth Poetry Collective, a contributor to the *Word of Mouth Anthology* (Blackstaff, 1992) which was translated into Russian and published in St Petersburg, and has produced English versions of poems by the St Petersburg poet Galina Gamper for a forthcoming parallel text. She is the author of two poetry collections from Summer Palace Press: *Banjaxed* (2001) and *The Nervous Flyer's Companion* (2010).

&

Hope Uchio is a daughter of Christian missionaries and has spent much of her adult life in Japan. Hope took care of her mother (in Japan) for over ten years. In *Regrets* she reflects on experiences she shared with her mother and expresses remorse. Hope is currently a full-time lecturer at a Japanese university and teaches courses in English and intercultural communication. Writing, for her, is a passion and a path to finding meaning in life. She is also happily married to a Japanese professor.

&

Alison Wassell, formerly a primary school teacher, is now an aspiring writer, voluntary charity shop worker and seeker of other gainful employment. Her contribution, *The Mother Thief* is a heavily fictionalised piece inspired by events surrounding her mother's death six years ago.

&

Janet Willoughby is a keen cook. She returned from a perplexing day in a nursing home as Practice Development Nurse, preventing the admission of an elderly frail resident. Needing to unwind, Janet wrote the *Enhancing Dementia Recipe:* it expresses her frustration and fears for vulnerable elderly people. Janet has worked in palliative care for more decades than she cares to admit – in hospices, the community and a general hospital. She currently loves being an educator, facilitator nurse at The Hospice of St Francis, Hertfordshire, and the NHS Health Education East of England ABC End of Life Education Programme.

Printed in Great Britain
by Amazon.co.uk, Ltd.,
Marston Gate.